LEARN W
HAVE WHA
HOW TO GET IT

Manifest
that
Miracle

LANA SHLAFER

ISBN: 978-19-5315300-5

Published by

LIFESTYLE
ENTREPRENEURS
P R E S S

If you are interested in publishing through Lifestyle Entrepreneurs Press, write to: *Publishing@LifestyleEntrepreneursPress.com*

Publications or foreign rights acquisition of our catalog books. Learn More: *www.LifestyleEntrepreneursPress.com*

Printed in the USA

*I dedicate this book to those who
dare to do the impossible.*

Contents

1:

Why Isn't the Law of Attraction Working for Me?

I bet you didn't grow up hearing about "manifesting" or "living your dream life."

Most people grew up in an environment where they were so focused on making it through life and surviving their family and school that they didn't think about "dreaming big" or feel like "everything is always working out." That's why the law of attraction is considered New Age even though it's basically what yogis shared over 5,000 years ago and what Jesus and Buddha taught. That's why it resonates so deeply within you. It goes beyond conditioning and straight into your heart and gut.

When I first learned about the law of attraction, I honestly thought it was a scam. Or worse, a religion or a cult. That was because it was so different from the ideas that I grew up with. Most of us heard things like this in our childhood:

- "No pain, no gain"
- "Money doesn't just grow on trees"
- "It's God's will and in God's hands"
- "Nothing good ever comes easy"
- "That's not possible"

And if you were extra "lucky" to be born in a family with generational trauma, you may have also heard pretty strong messages, not just about "reality," but about who you are. They may or may not have been said out loud, but you felt them, like:

- "You're lazy or stupid – not smart or talented enough"
- "You're not special – not worthy or deserving"
- "You're a burden – and owe me for taking care of you"
- "You're a failure – why can't you get it right?"
- "You're too much of this and that"
- "You're not enough and never will be enough"

Law of Attraction: A Way Out

The truth is most of us have some deep wounds stemming from childhood, and usually we're not even aware of the ways they impact our present-day self-talk, relationships, opportunities, etc. But despite all of these limiting beliefs that have been passed down to you generation after generation, you have still managed to discover the law of attraction. When you did, it gave you hope – hope that there is a way out of the bleakness and the perspective you were raised with. Hope that there is a way to end the chain of pain and start the cycle of healing, joy, and freedom.

The term "law of attraction" is credited to New Age philosophy. It is a belief system that draws a connection between the person's inner experience and the outer world they perceive. Although the law of attraction has become synonymous with positive thinking, metaphysical theories, and New Age thought, I think of the law of attraction as more of a mechanism that already exists and is always in motion.

I'm guessing you picked up this book because you've already read up on deliberate creation materials and tried out various methods of manifesting. I bet you've even seen some successes that felt amazing! Maybe you set your intention to find a parking space right in front of the store and you are now getting good at manifesting them all the time. Or maybe you got an unexpected check in the mail, or started meditating, and have felt much more present and calm.

The gratitude journals, visualizations, and vision boards may have helped take your life from OK to pretty good. You might love starting your days with more intention and be seeing the results of living more deliberately. Yet every time you try to focus on the thing that *really* matters to you, such as:

- manifesting a dream partner with whom you feel safe, seen, and supported
- manifesting enough money where you feel secure, free, and playful
- manifesting a successful career where you feel fulfilled, purposeful, and inspired

- manifesting health, fitness, and vitality so you feel good in your body daily
- manifesting a dream home, ideal job, book deal, exotic travel... the WOW dream

You find yourself stuck, disappointed, and wondering if this "manifesting stuff" is just a bunch of BS, or if there is something wrong with you so that you can't figure it out. You see other people "attracting" all this awesome stuff: your friend won a vacation, someone you saw on a YouTube video manifested $10,000 in a week, and you've seen inspiring stories of people creating something out of nothing. They share how it seemed impossible or difficult, yet here they are, living their dream.

You might be sitting here wondering when it's your turn. When will the law of attraction muses come to your neck of the woods and bless you? You're tired of working hard trying to manifest stuff and then not seeing the big result you want. You may have even picked up this book as a last resort to see if it really works.

Miracles Are Just Things That Haven't Happened Yet

I'm here to tell you what you want is possible. Your big vision, your WOW dreams, and your ambitious goals are not just possible – they are your destiny. But you won't get there while you feel small and unworthy, and your dreams feel so big. The key to learning how to mold your reality is understanding that your reality is formed by your perspective and that the only real limits are the ones you perceive.

Miracles are just things that haven't happened yet. After they happen, they are facts.

Think of Roger Banister, who broke the four-minute mile record. There were scientific articles written about how no human would be able to run a mile under four minutes—that it was impossible. Then he went and did it and it became a fact. Afterwards, many others did as well. The current record for a mile is three minutes and forty-three seconds.

So why was Roger able to break this mental and physical barrier in a way that is still talked about decades later? I haven't spoken to Roger personally, but over the fifteen years that I've been studying psychology, law of attraction, mindset, and human potential, I can promise you that he had three key things that allowed him to manifest the unbelievable:

1. **He had intention:** he focused on running the fastest he possibly could.
2. **He took action:** he trained with focus, intensity, and consistency.
3. **He loved what he was doing:** he trained in a sport that he loved.

This goes for any person who you've ever seen do something incredible. From the greatest athletes to tech innovators to YouTube stars, anyone who has achieved something big had to have these same three things:

1. They had intention: a clear unwavering focus that they returned to over and over.
   - They had a clear idea of their goal and used it as their North Star to keep moving in that direction.

- They didn't spend time worrying about others, feeling jealous, or complaining because that takes focus away from their intention.

2. They took action: they showed up consistently and deliberately.
   - They committed to the process, not the result, so they showed up consistently no matter what the outcome.
   - They had a plan or strategy and weren't doing things blind, so they were able to test and experiment with what worked best.
   - They weren't riding on emotions, faith, or hope – they were putting their attention on taking daily Inspired Action towards something they could control.

3. They loved what they were doing: they did something that was personally rewarding, valuable, or enjoyable.
   - They chose something they were willing to show up for in rain or shine, when it was fun and when it was not, because it intrinsically mattered to them.
   - Even those with an iron will might give up if they do not think that what they are doing matters much. So those who became miracle makers managed to find something that was valuable, fulfilling, and important enough that they were willing to eat the "crap sandwiches" that life occasionally served.

With a clear *intention* + enough *action*, you will *eventually* reach your goal. But whether you will be satisfied when you do is a whole other question.

Goal versus Miracle

There are plenty of people who reach their intentions and then feel more miserable than ever. Some even kill themselves (think of Robin Williams or Kate Spade). So there is an extra ingredient that is necessary to not only reach a goal, but to actually feel satisfied, happy, and fulfilled when you do – inspiration.

Inspiration literally means "in-spirit" or "in-connection with Spirit."

What is Spirit? I will be using the word Spirit or Source throughout the book as equivalent to the word God. You don't have to be religious or believe in God to recognize some sort of an organizing principle or universal energy that is beyond the physical realm. You can call it infinite intelligence or even nature. It doesn't matter what you call this idea—what matters is that you develop a direct connection with something that makes you feel like you are plugged into electricity and able to operate at optimal capacity.

When we are inspired or in connection with Spirit, we have access to all of ourselves: the part of us that is visible to the human eye and the part that is invisible that connects us to All-That-Is. When both of these parts of us – the physical and non-physical – work in harmony, we feel like we are whole, on purpose, and connected to endless energy of Source that powers us.

That's when thousands of action hours don't feel hard – they may feel strenuous, challenging, and intense, but they also feel satisfying, enjoyable, and rewarding. I wish there were different words for "hard" – one that symbolizes the "hard" when you are playing a video game you love or dancing or singing for hours until your body gives out because *you love it* versus the kind of "hard" that is concentration camp labor. There is an element of both "I chose this" and "this is choosing me" with things that we have a natural preference for or an inclination toward. When you feel inspired, you don't mind taking the steps toward your goal because you feel a gratification in the action. When you don't feel inspired, it feels like soul-less work – exhausting, tiring, and like pushing a boulder up a hill. This kind of hard ends up ultimately feeling futile and not worth the cost.

A good example of this is having a desire to get more fit and healthy. There are a gazillion ways to do so and each of them may have various degrees of appeal for each person. It kills me to see people force themselves to run five miles when they hate it or punish themselves with starvation diets that pain them. This is the draining, resistant, *hard* path. They suffer, struggle, and feel worse even if they get some results because there was so much sacrifice involved in the process. That feeling of sacrifice and suffering is a sign of not being "in-spirit" and, in essence, being disconnected from a part of yourself. That's why it feels so bad.

Instead, they could dance or walk instead of running. They could do ten-minute plyometric workouts twice a day instead of an hour run twice a week. They could join a group of friends to take classes or play sports. They could adjust their food intake slowly by finding more things they love that make their bodies feel good and focusing on what they are *adding* to their plates instead of what they are *removing*. They could have more sex, drink more water, and do more breathing exercises – all incredible metabolism boosters that can be highly enjoyable. They could take boat-loads of action and reach their goal in a way that increases their life force and enhances their life.

This path wouldn't feel like a sacrifice, it may not even feel like "work" at all!

Why would anyone choose the path of suffering when there are a million other ways to their goal? Because their mind limit won't let them see another way, even though plenty of other options exist. That's why a huge focus of this book is to help you open up your mind to new possibilities so you see the path of least resistance and most enjoyment to your goals. And that's why we will be focused on staying inspired – plugged into Source – so that we can recognize and take the actions that lead to massive results, incredible non-physical support, and unbelievable satisfaction. That's what creates miracles!

Inspired Intention + Inspired Action = Miracles

So why is any of this relevant to you today? Because in order to test the hypothesis that you can have anything you truly want, you'll need to understand what it takes to have it. Once you have the ingredients for a cake recipe, it's about experimenting to bake the perfect cake. That's exactly what this book is about.

I'm not here to give you a bunch of theory and tell you awesome success stories of other people who've done pretty dope things (though there will be a little bit of that for context). I'm here to show you practical tools that have worked for me and thousands of people so *you* can have results that feel miraculous. And I'm not just teaching you how to do this once – I hope to help you understand how you can apply these techniques to any area of your life to see massive shifts.

Miracle Maker

The unofficial goal I have for this book is that you realize all of this deliberate creation business is far simpler than you thought. I want you to feel like you've just found a magic wand and now you can grant yourself any wish you want! But I also want to make sure that you're aware what you *want* and what you *get* may be slightly (or hugely) different – and that this is *great*!

I want you to not just be able to get what you want, but to love what you get and be able to extract the gift in any situation. I want you to feel bigger than any problem – so much so that you stop seeing problems altogether and instead see opportunities. What if every tombstone felt like a stepping-stone and you felt powerful and free no matter what the circumstances?

It's possible for you to feel unconditionally worthy: before and after a million dollars, before and after your dream partner, and before and after *that* miracle! My goal for this book is to teach you how to feel supported and guided so you no longer feel alone, lost, or disappointed for long. Then you will enjoy amazing daily miracles that can delight, inspire, and amaze you along the way to the big manifestations.

I'm so excited for you to begin learning how to build the Miracle Mindset so you can manifest your desires and feel like a miracle maker in your life!

2:

How I Turned Pain into Gain

When most people meet me, they see a blonde, happy California girl. Unlike my Filipino husband, I rarely get questions like, "Where are you *really* from?" The irony is that he's the American who spent his whole life in the US and I'm the immigrant.

I was born in a town called Tomsk in central Siberia. Everything you heard about Siberia is true – it's super cold and remote. But it's also beautiful. Tomsk is a pretty cosmopolitan town, with four educational institutions and about 700,000 residents.

When I was born in 1981, Russia was still part of the USSR. It was during my childhood that communism fell apart and all the Soviet Republics broke into separate countries. I come from a Jewish father and a Belorussian-Ukrainian mother who grew up in Kazakhstan. So I spent most of every year in Tomsk and then my summers in Kazakhstan.

I was always headstrong, independent, and stubborn, but super sensitive. This resulted in me having uncontrollable fits of crying and "acting out" for a lot of my childhood. My parents still tell stories of how, when I wouldn't get something I wanted, I would scream on the floor, pounding my fists for hours until I'd exhaust myself. Looking back, what I wanted was love, acceptance, and presence. But my parents couldn't give it to me – they were crawling out of their skin trying to survive anti-Semitism, poverty, generational trauma, and an oppressive regime. They did the absolute best they could and gave everything they had to my brother and me, but it was still a tough life.

Growing up in this way made me very jaded about life. The message I got from my environment early on was that no one would love someone like me – I was too demanding, too opinionated, and just too much to handle. Often I felt like a burden to my parents and that translated to deep thorns of unworthiness and pangs of abandonment within. The communist culture and educational system did not appreciate my zest for initiative and passion for justice, either. I was constantly told I had to be a "good" girl and do as I was told. My family, culture, and environment shaped the way I looked at the world and determined how I lived until I realized that I could change my perspective and therefore my whole life.

Generation of Survivors

From where I stood twenty years ago, it seemed completely impossible for me to live a life of ease or feel head-over-heels in love with myself and life. Both of my familial lines were dysfunctional. However, dysfunction was totally normal in Russia and surviving was the pinnacle of success.

I come from generations of survivors.

My paternal grandfather's name was Zinoviy, but I knew him as Ded Zyama. I grew up with stories of how he and his twin brother became orphans in WWII. When the Nazi army came to their Yiddish village, they had to escape. They ran for three days straight and my grandfather would tell me stories of how he learned to sleep while still walking.

When they got separated from their parents, my grandpa had to rely on street smarts to make sure he and his twin survived. They found an orphanage, lied, and said they were twelve instead of fourteen (fourteen was the cut-off age for orphanages). They had to learn Russian, but most importantly, they had to learn how to survive without much food and in the roughest environment imaginable.

My grandfather would tell me stories of sneaking into people's gardens to steal potatoes from the ground (which they'd eat raw). He would always tell it with a sly smile on his face, boasting that he was good at running away from the owners, who would shoot them with guns loaded with salt pellets. He'd proudly say that he'd only been shot once and it was worth it because stealing those fruits and veggies kept him and his brother alive during a tough post-war time.

His stories about the hardships he'd lived were usually full of pride and an attitude of positivity. Even when he spoke of his first return to the village where he grew up, he would find a way to make something horrific seem like a lesson with meaning. He found out that all the elders who were too old or ill to leave before the Nazis came were gathered in my great-grandmother's house and burned alive by the German army. When he stood at the ashes of what used to be his childhood home, he vowed to make something of himself and his life.

And boy, did he! He managed to get accepted to engineering school in Siberia, but he didn't have money for the train to get there, so he snuck on the train and hid the entire three-day trip – even sometimes riding on the roof – to avoid the conductor. Once he got situated in the university, my grandfather was ready to get married. So when he laid eyes on my grandmother – the first eligible Jewish girl he met – he proposed right away. Four days later, they were married, and less than a year later, they welcomed their first baby boy, Alexander, to the world. That was my dad.

My paternal grandmother's name was Maria, or Baba Masha, as I called her. She was born to Jewish parents in Leningrad (now St. Petersburg) and went through the worst siege in history. The siege of Leningrad was a prolonged military **blockade** of all roads to the city, so no supplies could get in from 1941 to 1943. Nearly three million people endured it and just under half of them died, starving or freezing to death during the cold winters. My grandmother and her family were some of the few survivors.

I know my grandmother endured horrors, such as seeing corpses on the street, kids whose parents died, and parents whose kids died – and they were not even able to bury them because they were too weak to dig a grave. She rarely spoke of her childhood and I know little about her life, mostly because she spent most of her life in bed.

She suffered from debilitating depression. She was so severely bipolar that she was hospitalized multiple times, had to stop working as an English teacher, and was a pretty unfit mother. My dad remembers times when she was in good spirits – when she'd cook, sing, or teach him English. But the majority of the time she was in bed with a glassy look on her face, crying or sleeping.

There Is Always a Way

My grandfather once told me a story of how he had to give my dad and his brother (who were three and one at the time) to temporary foster care because he was working, my grandmother couldn't take care of them, and he couldn't find anyone else. One day, he came to see them and saw his one-year-old son, my uncle, covered in scales from eczema and lying in excrement from not being changed. So he decided that was it. Within a few days, he miraculously found someone to take care of his kids, got them out of the foster care home, and vowed to never take them there again.

He told me this story before he died and even then, he had a mischievous smile on his face. He said he had to get creative so he started showing affection to a woman who he thought would be a good caretaker. She was the one who helped watch my dad and uncle as kids. My grandfather never sugarcoated the tough parts of life, but he wanted to instill in me the skill of looking for solutions instead of staring at problems.

Ded Zyama was an instrumental person in my life because he was the person I was closest to growing up. He taught me how to survive. According to him, the key was, "Don't take anything so seriously that you can't find the humor in it. When you lose perspective, you lose."

Ironically, this is one key tenet of the law of attraction that most people miss, and that's why they don't see the results they want.

It was through learning how to move through my own depression and misery that I realized the truth of the popular quote: "It's all going to be OK in the end. If it's not OK, it's not the end." Now I *choose* to see it all as OK – I color everything that happens as good and that's how I can derive the good from any situation.

Don't Ask for Smaller Problems, Ask for a Bigger You

When you let something feel bigger than you, it's out of your control. But when you feel bigger than any problem, you can achieve anything.

My dad took this to heart as well. He was sick a lot in his childhood and was bullied. But he didn't let it hold him down. He worked hard in school and decided to get a PhD in Mathematics – notoriously the hardest degree to receive, especially with rampant anti-Semitism in the Soviet Union, which made it even more difficult for a Jewish grad student.

He developed resilience and the capacity to dream the impossible. He had the kind of intensity of vision that is only born out of pain. It was this drive to survive and create a better life for his kids that drove him to look for ways to get his family out of an oppressive communist regime.

I remember my dad being weird in my childhood: practicing yoga from contraband books, eating a vegetarian diet (unheard of in Russia then), and teaching Esperanto. Esperanto is the most successful artificial language. It was created in 1887 by Dr. Zamenhof, a pacifist and dreamer who came up with a simple language that everyone could easily learn as a second language to communicate with anyone in the world. Esperanto never took off as *the* international language, but an estimated ten to twenty million people around the world speak it.

My parents met when my dad was teaching Esperanto (for fun while in grad school) and my mom came to his classes. So my brother and I grew up in the Esperanto community, speaking both Esperanto and Russian from birth. This is super rare and only a handful of native Esperanto speakers have ever existed.

My dad learned Esperanto as a way to communicate with the outside world, which was very difficult under the extreme communist censorship. He wanted to get out of Russia, so he started applying for citizenship anywhere he could: Israel, Canada, the US. During the early nineties, the US government was giving out green cards to a select few highly-educated Eastern Europeans of Jewish descent. This wave of immigration was later called a "brain-drain."

The one requirement was to have someone in America vouch for the character of the applicants. My dad had one Esperanto friend who had emigrated from USSR to California in 1979. Luckily this friend vouched for us and we were one of the fortunate families that were granted a green card. But the truth is this wasn't about luck – my dad would never describe it as such, but rather that he systematically and deliberately worked toward a miracle.

In 1993, we landed in San Francisco and started our new life in America. I was twelve years old when my old life as I knew it ended. I came to a place I'd only seen in movies to start a whole new existence. I was sad to leave my family and friends in Russia, but I didn't really have much of a choice. Of course, in retrospect this was the most amazing turn of events and gave me so many opportunities I would have never had otherwise.

But the first few years of my life in America were rough – I was bullied for how I looked, for my broken English, and for being super poor. I went from being a popular kid in Russia to being the "loser" in middle school. This was one of the toughest times of my life, but it taught me valuable lessons about humility, compassion, inclusivity, and self-worth that are now a part of who I am as an individual.

So it is with absolute certainty that I know that what doesn't kill me makes me stronger. And it's now my mission in this world to help those who are ready to thrive to turn their pain into massive gain.

Wound Mates

My maternal grandfather, Ded Vasya, and my maternal grandmother, Baba Nina, met after he got out of the army and she had just finished university. They fell in love, got married, had my mom, and then moved to Kazakhstan for life in a bigger city with more job opportunities.

My grandfather got a job with the police and my grandmother got a job as a secretary at a printing company. They did the best they could raising their three kids. Life in the USSR was brutal and my mom had a troubled childhood. The details are blurry, but let's just say there was enough trauma for her to want to build a better life and be on her own.

Higher education was a priority for my mom – she was determined to make it out of her environment and make a difference in the world. So she studied hard and applied to the best universities. At seventeen years old, she moved five thousand miles away from her home to go to university in Tomsk, Siberia. It was there she met my dad and saw all the qualities she was looking for in a partner: intelligence, passion, drive. They dated and got married soon after.

She was younger and idealized him. Like all relationships, they came together as "wound mates." They triggered the heck out of each other and I spent my childhood watching them fight. I knew they loved my brother and me dearly, but it was difficult for me.

A Losing Battle

When we moved to the US, I was cut off from my extended family and more on my own than ever. Yet I also now had incredible opportunities available to me. I was determined to create a life that my parents hoped for and to pay them back for the sacrifices they made. I did my best to deal with being bullied in middle school. I sat by myself at lunch for months and would cry myself to sleep every night. Then the next day I'd get up and survive one more day.

I tried to adapt and conform to the American culture, but I struggled through high school and college. I developed depression and a binge eating habit. Somehow I still managed to graduate from UC Berkeley with a 3.8 GPA. In the process, I tapped into the fighter in me that so many in my lineage had to be in order to survive – bring it on, I can conquer it! The one thing that kept me going was the dream that after I finished college, I'd get an awesome job and finally have the freedom and purpose I wanted.

I worked insanely hard and got five job offers out of college. I chose Citigroup and worked in corporate and investment banking in the tech sector. I was making tons of money and jet-setting around the world, supposedly living the dream. But inside, I felt absolutely wretched. As I continued binge eating, self-loathing, and suffering from anxiety, and depression, thoughts of running away to India and living in an ashram seemed like the only way out.

This was a dark period of hopelessness, sadness, and impenetrable loneliness. It was at this time that I decided, *screw it.* I'd rather die than live as a pale and unrecognizable version of myself. I had been trying to live out the American dream and create the security my parents wanted for me, but I was absolutely miserable and lost. This was when the internet was taking off and I'd see some of my peers traveling the world, doing what they loved, and looking so happy on social media – so why was I so damn depressed and broken, unable to figure it out?

I was tired of the war raging within me. Fighting yourself is always a losing battle. No matter which part of you wins, you are left feeling torn up. I had already been practicing yoga and meditation for a few years by then and loved the oasis of peace I experienced through the practice. So I decided I had to leave the soul-less, slave-driving world of banking and look for work with meaning and joy.

A Way Out

I did something totally unprecedented in my family – gave myself some time to discover what I wanted. I had some savings, so I quit Citigroup and moved from San Francisco to Los Angeles without having a job lined up.

Then I went on a ten-day *silent* meditation retreat – it almost killed me as the demons within all came up to the surface. But on the seventh day, I experienced true inner harmony for the first time in my life. It was revolutionary. I never wanted this feeling to end.

I started opening up to the idea that there is an organizing principle for life and that it is possible to experience oneness and connection to something bigger than me, bigger than my reality, maybe even bigger than all of the physical realm. I realized that this connection to my spirit and to Source was all that I need to feel happy and fulfilled. I no longer needed to control every detail just to feel OK. I no longer needed someone to give me love or validation. I no longer needed to keep running and surviving. I could stop and just be. That felt like a *huge* relief.

Moreover, I felt as if I were truly waking up when I recognized that everything in my outer reality was a reflection of my inner state. Who knew that the world isn't just "well, that's the way things are?" When I realized the possibility that the reality I was seeing was one giant mirror, my mind was blown! Because if that's true, then I hold the key to creating what I want—nothing else.

I wouldn't frown in the mirror and expect my reflection to smile back at me. So why was I feeling so miserable on the inside and yet expecting people, situations, and accomplishments in my life to smile back at me with happiness and fulfillment?

This was a huge realization that gave me the ability to shift everything in my life. I stopped chasing the manifestations I thought I *needed* to feel good and just focused on feeling good. I know that sounds simple, but it's pretty damn revolutionary in practice. It liberated me to focus on the things I can control – my thoughts, emotions, perspectives, and habits – and let go of the need to control the external world.

21

Why Didn't Anyone Tell Me This Before?

After that, things unfolded pretty quickly.

I found a job as a success coach for college students. I received training in life coaching and met inspiring colleagues who were passionate about self-improvement and global impact. I had already been in therapy since college, but now I started working with a life coach and reading every self-help book I could get my hands on.

After I left that job, I got certified as a yoga teacher (RYT-500) and started teaching and running yoga teacher trainings. I discovered Wayne Dyer, Abraham Hicks, Michael Beckwith, and other spiritual teachers. I started going to Agape Spiritual Center and, for the first time in my life, opened up to the idea of God in a real way.

I had so many incredible healing experiences and saw such huge shifts in my life. That's when all of these ideas were no longer theoretical – I saw experiential evidence in my life that change is possible. I recognized that everything is energy and that I create with my thoughts. I realized that my perspective is key to my fulfillment and that I can manifest anything I want. This changed my life forever and I couldn't believe that no one told me this before!

The new friends I was making believed in infinite possibilities. They took leaps, watched wings appear, and soared. Over time it became more and more normal to live this way daily. But there were still deep-seated feelings of shame, blame, and pain that I couldn't seem to shake. I felt like I was still running away from feeling not enough, too much, unlovable, and like a failure.

When I enrolled in an MA in Counseling at the Institute of Transpersonal Psychology (now Sophia University), I dove into an intense and life-altering period of shadow work. I was determined to let go of fighting myself and learn to love and accept myself at the deepest levels possible. I was making amazing progress, experiencing deep healing, and learning so much about how pain can be a gift... and then life happened, again.

Boom, Bam, Pow

In the middle of grad school, I got engaged to my on-again, off-again boyfriend of two and a half years. A month later, we found out we were pregnant... with *twins*! This turned my whole world upside down. All of a sudden it wasn't just me – I was about to have a family.

I left grad school and focused on practicing everything I knew to have a healthy pregnancy and a wonderful birth. We relocated to southern California and I looked for prenatal care there. Most women have already chosen their doctor and figured out a birth plan by thirty weeks of pregnancy, so I was a little concerned. Moreover, I had been reading books about birthing written by midwives, yoga teachers, and psychologists and was really considering having a home birth with a midwife. In the stories about home births, the women went through amazing vision quests, discovering their own strength and softness, molding into the divine feminine.

I wanted one of those experiences where I was empowered to let my body birth, to bond with my partner, and to feel the primordial creative force coming through us as we journeyed together with our babies through the transition from the unseen world into the material world. I wanted to feel everything – yes, everything – the joy, the fear, the pain. I wanted to feel what millions of women have gone through since time began. Nowhere in this vision of mine did I see bright lights, hospital gowns, being hooked up to an IV and immobilized, being told what to do and when to do it...

I faced resistance from some friends and acquaintances after sharing with them my desire to give birth at home, so I stopped talking about it except with a few select friends who were supportive and encouraging. My husband and I had to put aside the naysayers' words about the impossibility of a vaginal delivery, the hopelessness of finding a midwife when I was seven months pregnant, the difficulty of birthing drug-free, etc. Never had I had to rely on my intuition more and trust that if I could conceive it, I could achieve it.

Miracles and Misery

You can read more about my birth story on my blog, but suffice it to say it was a truly miraculous experience. We ended up having an extraordinary six-day home birth with my twin son and daughter born thirty-three hours apart. Yes, they have different birthdays!

The number of angels, human and non-physical, that showed up to support us during the pregnancy and birth showed me the miracles possible when there is an *Inspired Intention + Inspired Action*. I couldn't believe I did it! We did it! We manifested an extraordinary birth of two healthy, beautiful babies at home. I felt victorious in a way I'm not sure I'll ever be able to top again.

My children taught me what it's like to go beyond imagination and manifest the impossible! But after the glorious birth, we had two kids to care for around the clock as first-time parents. The first months of the twins' lives were difficult and required me to expand my capacity to receive support and surrender to what I couldn't control. My husband and I fought so badly under all the financial, physical, and emotional stress that we were at the brink of a divorce. We were in debt, we had two kids to take care of, and there didn't seem to be a way to make things easier.

This was another pivotal time in my life when I had to imagine and believe that there was a way for things to get better even though I felt disheartened and stuck. I felt like this was another turning point – I could have shrunk back into the survival, hustle, suffering, and misery that was so normalized in my childhood. Or I could expand into this new version of myself who could learn to thrive, trust, love, and take risks even when things seemed bleak.

I made time for therapy, paid money we didn't have for a nanny a few hours a week to have time for myself, and swallowed my pride to ask for help from friends and family. All of this felt totally unimaginable to me until I hit my version of rock bottom. I had such a bad milk duct infection from nursing that I ended up hospitalized and had surgery.

During four days in the hospital without seeing my newborns, I had a lucid moment: *I gotta go back to practicing what I preach and take care of myself and ask for support. Even if it's vulnerable, embarrassing, or terrifying – in times of crisis, my priority has to be my alignment and well-being.* It got me focused on creating an Inspired Intention—feeling rested, supported, and happy as a mama. And got me to take unprecedented Inspired Action—ask for help and receive it even when my old programming was telling me that I am a bad mother if I can't do it all myself or if I prioritize my needs above my husband's or my kids'.

This turned the "impossible" situation around – I started feeling full of myself again, my marriage was improving, and my kids felt more manageable and even life-giving.

Leap of Faith

When the twins were one, I resumed teaching yoga and started working part-time as a project manager, but people kept asking me to share about our birth experience and about how I was able to stay positive in the face of so many challenges. So I started doing workshops here and there. Then I started seeing my yoga clients as coaching clients.

Eventually I decided to take the leap and go into my coaching practice full-time. But I had one problem: I didn't have the money to invest in my new business. We were still living paycheck-to-paycheck and paying off credit card and school debt. But I also couldn't imagine working full-time, going back to finish my master's degree to be a therapist, or doing anything else.

So I did something that my parents forbid me to do. I cashed out my 401K to give myself $40K as my "salary" and seed money to invest in coaching training, business courses, and professional development to start my business. This was in 2012, and looking back, that was absolutely the *right* decision for me. I went *all in* on my dream, so life could go all in with me. The rest is history!

I went to Abraham-Hicks workshops and cruises, and I spoke with Infinite Intelligence in the hot seats. People loved my discussions with Abraham, more and more people were reading my blogs, and I built a beautiful website and learned how to do online coaching (instead of in-person). Now my clients could be anywhere in the world!

I created my first online course in 2014 and those participants saw such epic results that they started telling everyone they knew about my work. I found so much power in being in a MasterMind group based on the principles from Napoleon Hill that I started offering my unique MasterMind programs and they sold like hotcakes.

My manifesting challenges took off and the participants were seeing so many shifts that they were asking for more courses and programs! My business grew, my team grew, I crossed the six-figure mark in my business within three years and kept growing, but slowly I was starting to feel overworked.

A Smack in the Face!

Sure, I had over 20,000 participants go through my manifesting challenges, but I was getting depleted. The hardest part was the constant revolving door of contractors and team members in my company. My business felt especially difficult after we had our third baby. I did a big course launch when he was six months old. At that point, my husband was traveling all the time for his job in education sales. We hired a live-in nanny and got lots of help, but no matter how much help I had, I felt tired and overwhelmed.

During this big launch, I had 8,000 participants in the manifesting challenge. I spent more money than ever on my team and advertising and when I didn't see the results I wanted, I entered a few days of deep depression. I wondered if I was not cut out to run a business. Sure, I was great at the work I did, but I didn't know how to be a great manager. As my expenses and team members grew, I felt more and more pressure to keep producing so I had less time for creating for the joy of it.

I also wondered if I could keep going in my marriage. Sure, I loved my husband and he loved me, but we seemed to be on different pages. He wanted to keep growing in his company and didn't mind that he traveled every other week... and I didn't want to be a solo parent during those times. Life was feeling utterly overwhelming and I felt super stuck.

My kids needed me to be present and a loving parent, my team was depending on me to produce so we could keep the company growing, my clients and program participants expected programs and courses that over-delivered... and I... just... couldn't... anymore. I felt stupid that with everything I know and teach, I somehow still moved into hard action and away from inspiration. I was judging myself for pushing myself so much when I *should* have known better.

Thank goodness this wasn't my first rodeo and I knew that this was a "come-to-Jesus" moment that would change my life. I knew the way out of this situation was to practice what I preached on a whole new level. So I took the focus back to creating more alignment as if my life depended on it (because it did):

- I prioritized my daily alignment practice to connect to my soul and to Source.
- I carved out space to be creative and feel nurtured above anything else.
- I let go of most of my team and simplified my business.

- I expressed fully how I felt to my husband and gave him an ultimatum, saying we needed to get on the same page or go our separate ways.

This was not easy. There was so much momentum to keep going, going, going from my old programming. To not rock the boat in my marriage. To minimize what was happening because on the surface, I had everything I wanted: a loving partner, three healthy happy kids, a thriving business... It was scary to let that go. I worried we'd end up in debt again, I'd hurt those I love, and I'd be a failure.

I faced all of the fears head-on. I knew there was nowhere to run anymore. I held myself as I cried and released. I doubled up on healers and coaches to offer support. I asked for and received more love and help from my friends and family. As difficult as it was to pause, I knew that the alternative was way harder. I had to stop, drop, and realign to my Inspired Intention.

Breakdown to Breakthrough

And the world didn't end. For a minute, we did have some debt (huge tax bills were definitely a new level, new devil kind of problem), but I saw it as a gift. I was getting a loan from the universe to take care of myself and build a new life. So I felt grateful. (How is that for "coloring it good"?!)

My husband and I had many heart-to-heart discussions and experienced a deeper healing of childhood wounds. We created an amazing vision for what we wanted *our* life to look like. We wanted to travel, show our kids the world, be location-independent, and homeschool. We thought it would take us a few years to actually bring this vision to life, but when you are a miracle maker like me, buckle up because things happen at lightning speed!

Within nine months of taking a vacation to Puerto Rico to consider it as a possible future home, we were boarding a plane to go live there. It was truly miracle after miracle and nudge after nudge from the universe that got us to land in our new island life in 2019. My husband got laid off and received severance, which bought him time to discover what he wanted to do next and homeschool our kids! I connected with the most incredible entrepreneurial community in Puerto Rico and have seen so many personal and business breakthroughs that it would take me another book to enumerate them all.

My business is doing better than ever with me working less and enjoying everything I do more. My marriage has reached a higher level of intimacy, passion, connection, and fulfillment than I *ever* imagined a relationship could have. My kiddos are thriving in their new life and are loving the adventures, travel, and massive learning they get to experience.

In my husband, kids, and my work, I found mirrors that constantly show me opportunities to heal, reveal, and soar.

Happiness beyond Imagination

I feel truly happy. I wake up with a deep feeling of satisfaction. My inner wisdom guides me in every way. I go to sleep with waves of fulfillment washing over me, in infinite appreciation of all the elements of my life that make it so extraordinary and meaningful. My mind is at peace. My heart feels full. My body is fitter and healthier than ever. I am living my dreams and now creating even juicier visions!

Challenges don't scare me – they thrill me. When personal tragedies strike or global catastrophes occur, I don't dismiss or resist what's happening. I use the tools in this book to find meaning, value, and gifts in every situation. I know that within every adversity lies the seed of opportunity, and I can rise not despite the problems, but because of them.

I'm writing this to you while in mandatory quarantine for the Coronavirus outbreak. While this global pandemic has been difficult, painful, tragic, and a great cause for concern, it's also a great cause for change. Change is inevitable. Evolution is essential. Suffering is optional. And we each get to choose whether we suffer or thrive as the world transforms.

When I realized that there is nothing bigger than me and I have the tools to make the most out of any experience, I fully stepped into my power. I created the unbelievable and lived the impossible. I have manifested so many miracles and I am here to help others do the same – not just in theory, but in practice. As in, a mate in your bed, money in your bank, purpose in your life, and, most importantly, a strong sense of empowerment, fulfillment, and joy.

If I can do it, given where I come from, anyone can.

3:

The Miracle Mindset

Merriam-Webster gives this as the definition of a miracle:

Miracle (noun)

1. an extraordinary event manifesting divine intervention in human affairs
2. an extremely outstanding or unusual event, thing, or accomplishment
3. a divinely natural phenomenon experienced humanly as the fulfillment of spiritual law.

You mostly hear about miracles in religion when a saint or God performs something so unbelievable that it can only be described as supernatural. Because I grew up non-religious (religion was banned in Communist Russia), I didn't have any previous associations with the words "miracle" or "manifesting." As I went on to experience things that could only be described as divine and supernatural, I couldn't find any other word to describe them except "miraculous."

Because I expanded my mindset, did various manifesting practices, and applied the law of attraction deliberately, I knew that *I* created the miracles. I had help from the expanded part of me, Spirit, but let's be clear. I was the one who called in this support. I was the one who learned how to perceive it, receive it, and amplify it.

I also understood that resistance is healthy, natural, and necessary for manifesting (and you will too, soon!). Problems, challenges, and hurdles were there as useful parts of my journey, not detours or unwanted tangents. So it was really odd for me to enter law of attraction circles and hear people feel so disempowered when things didn't go as expected.

Have-Do-Be or Be-Do-Have?

So many people hope for a manifestation. They pray for a miracle. They wish and wait for the bad stuff to end and for circumstances to change so they can finally feel happy. Most people want to *have* what they want so they can *do* what they want in order to *be* who they want to be.

But that's backwards. That's not how this reality works. You must first *be* a match to that reality in order to *do* what you dream and *have* what you want.

To have freedom, you must choose to *feel* free. To have abundance, you must find a way to *feel* abundant. To have happiness and satisfaction, you've got to find a way to *feel* them now, along the journey, not when you get "there."

Where is this mysterious "there" anyway? Our world is highly interpretative. To one person, having a million dollars is a dream. But to a billionaire, it's a nightmare. To one person, having cancer was the worst thing that could've happened to them. Yet to another, it was the greatest turn of events that transformed their life in ways they never imagined. To one person, conceiving a child is a huge wish come true and to another, getting pregnant is a tragedy.

Everything is relative. Think in your life when you achieved the things you wanted... did you stay satisfied forever? Or did you go right on to wanting the next thing? OK, I've got a husband who loves me now... on to the next problem to fixate on, worry about, and mull over. It's a never-ending chase after the moving target of goals that are outside of you.

So if getting *there* isn't the point, and even if you get *there* you won't be happy (for long), then what is the point?

Choose Joy

The point is who you become in the process. The point is to feel like a miracle maker anywhere, anytime, and under any circumstances. That's what the Miracle Mindset is all about.

As trite as it may sound, the joy really is in the journey. It's not about *where* you are along the journey—it's about how you *feel* about where you are that matters. Your reality is all about how you experience the situations around you and much less about the actual situations. I could give you a million examples, but here is one that I like to think about when I think things are unequivocally bad and no one can possibly interpret them otherwise.

Nelson Mandela was in jail for twenty-seven years. He was persecuted, locked up, and forced to do prison labor. He didn't get to go to his mother's funeral. He didn't see his kids grow up. I don't think anyone would wish this kind of an experience for themselves. And yet he was able to find alignment with his situation. Just like author and psychiatrist Viktor Frankl describes in his book *Man's Search for Meaning*, "Everything can be taken from a man but one thing: the last of the human freedoms – to choose one's attitude in any given set of circumstances, to choose one's own way."

Each of us is born with free will, but not many of us recognize or exercise this freedom. Just like in the case of Nelson Mandela and Viktor Frankl, miracles are possible when you find meaning – and maybe even a gift – in any situation. They chose to *feel* free even when imprisoned. That's what allowed them to *do* incredible things and then to *have* a massive positive impact on the world. I call this the ability to *color it good*.

If all circumstances are inherently neutral, then they only have the value you ascribe to them. However you describe a situation is what you will derive from it. If you learn how to color it good, you will derive the good from it.

This approach isn't for the faint of heart. This isn't law of attraction 'lite.' The Miracle Mindset is for those who want to learn how to let go of controlling outer circumstances and how to gain the capacity to manifest miracles and direct their destiny.

You Are Bad at Knowing What Will Make You Happy

Now let me give you an example of a situation that is supposedly unequivocally good. Who wouldn't want to win the lottery? Who wouldn't think it's absolutely miraculous to just start getting money every month? I mean, you'd think everyone would see it as a great manifestation.

Turns out, everyone except for the lottery winners would see it that way. There have been numerous studies by researchers that indicate little to no uptick in happiness or fulfillment after the initial period of winning the lottery. This is sometimes described as a hedonic adaptation, which is the tendency to get used to things that were once rare and exhilarating, and no longer experience a positive reaction to them.

Humans are also notoriously bad at accurately predicting what will make them happy. Psychologists call this affective forecasting. The most common answer for what would make you happier is: "more money." But studies have proven that a shorter commute, more travel, or having more free time actually moved the needle for fulfillment more than cash.

So if we

- don't actually know what will make us happier
- don't feel happier when we get what we want
- can find freedom and happiness in any circumstance

...then wouldn't it be a natural conclusion that what creates a meaningful, satisfying, extraordinary life is *not* chasing manifestations or miracles—it's becoming someone who can see the good in any situation and derive the miracle in it?

The best part? You can have your cake and eat it too!

In one of my famous hot seats with Abraham Hicks, Abraham told me, "Now that you know it's about how you feel and you can create that feeling on demand, guess you're just gonna have to suck it up and receive the matching manifestations because they will follow!" You see, you can focus on feeling fulfilled now and be excited about more to come. I'm not a monk renouncing material possessions – I love fancy champagne and luxurious surroundings – and I'm not proposing you become one, either.

You Can Have It All

You can have endless manifestations, luxuries, and whatever else you desire – as long as you recognize that it's for the joy of it and not to fill a void, and as long as you aren't trying to prove your worthiness or find some kind of eternal happiness in stuff.

Happiness is in the chase. Miracles are the perspective shifts that prove that you are a powerful, deliberate creator. So what is the Miracle Mindset?

It's a proven process that can take you from "I have a vision" to "I have arrived" over and over again. In this book, we will explore many different practices, tools, and perspectives that can be used to deliberately create something that feels unattainable right now. As long as you recognize that you will most likely arrive in a different place than you originally thought – and allow for the possibility of something so much better and more magical – let's dive into the overview of what it takes to manifest miracles.

Step 1: Assess

To get going where you want to go, you must start with knowing where you are and how you got here. This step is the equivalent of a GPS determining your current location so that when you program in your desired destination, it can give you the shortest route there. Once you know your mode of transportation (walking, bike, car, plane, etc.) and know how to operate all the equipment, you just need to follow the directions to get where you want to go.

In Chapter 4, we will explore formative life experiences – the pain and the successes that have shaped your self-view and world-view. This will give you clarity (and maybe even forgiveness and peace) on why you are where you are. It will also get you super clear on what you truly want. This clarity on the essence of what you want and why you want it will be a powerful North Star as you journey to creating incredible miracles and epic fulfillment!

Step 2: Allow

After you've honestly assessed where you are and what got you there, there is one more step before we can head to your desired destination. You must be available to the miracles you're asking for. That means you have to learn how to have space in your mind, heart, soul, and life to listen to the divine guidance.

You've got to learn to hear the directions clearly and be open to adjusting the route in case there is something blocking the path. Once you identify what resistance feels like and learn to work with it instead of fighting against it, you'll be able to hear and follow clear inner guidance. This is what we cover in Chapter 5.

You will be enjoying the journey so much, you won't be as concerned with "how long until I get there?" Instead, you'll be having so much magic in your daily life, you won't care when you get "there!"

Step 3: Imagine, Speak, Write, Create

The next step is finding the best ways for you to clearly identify, envision, and embody your desire. In Chapters 6 through 9, we will explore various modes of visioning and ways to live out your intentions in your life today. We will cover Guided Imagery Visioning, Written Visioning, Spoken Visioning, and Creative Expression Visioning. We will discuss what they are, who they work best for, when and how to use them, and why they are essential for manifesting miracles.

Think of all of these manifesting exercises as entering the parallel reality you prefer. These powerful techniques aren't making the manifestations happen – they are creating a bridge so you can cross to the reality where you are already living your desires. We are all unique and have different tastes and preferences – so consider these visioning methods as a big buffet where you can try everything once and then go back for seconds on the dishes you found most delicious and satisfying!

Step 4: Evaluate and Celebrate

This is maybe the most important step, because I don't want you to "believe" or "hope" that what I'm saying works. I want you to *prove* to yourself unequivocally that this method produces results. It's not enough to just see a delicious meal when you're hungry; the gratification is in the eating and digesting of it. Then, you spend the rest of your life remembering this epic meal and extract endless satisfaction out of it!

So we will do an honest assessment of what worked, what didn't, and why. We'll assess our hypotheses and whether you found a causation or correlation between practicing the Miracle Mindset and actual improvements in your life. We'll identify the progress and celebrate it, because celebrations attract more manifestations and life is better when we feel grateful and show it!

We will also address common blocks and next steps you can take to improve this process each time you do it. So get excited about dreaming even bigger, feeling even better, and crossing off more bucket-list items! If you are ready and eager to create an extraordinary event, manifest divine intervention, upgrade your mindset, and up-level your life, let's dive in!

The Big Ask

I do have a big ask from you before we begin. I'm going to ask you to do something that might feel difficult or even impossible: suspend your judgement and go all in.

You will reap what you sow. If you go into this book as a dabbler, you'll get a little dribble in results. If you go into this process as a skeptic, you'll get more skeptical the deeper you go. If you go into this experiment convinced it won't work, then you will self-fulfill this prophecy. The human mind is a powerful thing and your first lesson begins right now.

I'm going to ask you to get a journal or piece of paper and write out and sign the agreement below. In this agreement, I'm asking you to commit to doing the processes outlined in this book as if your life depended on it. Because your life does depend on it. You wouldn't have picked up this book if you didn't want to experience or create something extraordinary that isn't here yet. You wouldn't be reading these words if you didn't know that there is *more* possible for you, that you can have a bigger impact, heal at a deeper level, and manifest more miraculous dreams.

So this is the chance to turn back. You can put this book down or throw it in the trash and go on with your life as usual. Or you can take a leap of faith and try the exercises in this book that may change your life forever. Fifty percent of the change begins with a decision. Without the decision, there is no change. With the decision, you are halfway there.

So decide right now that you are going to carve out the time to read this book and complete each of the exercises in the next thirty days. Commit to going *all in* on this experiment and giving yourself a chance to learn, grow, heal, reveal, and soar like never before.

Please write this out on a piece of paper and sign it:

I have big visions and dreams and I'm ready to bring them to reality. I am committing to temporarily suspending my judgements and doing the processes described in this book. I will carve out time daily to read the chapters and practice the exercises to the best of my ability.

When doubts, fears, or self-limits come up, I commit to giving myself a hug and saying or writing: "I'm open. I'm ready. I've got this." When I feel behind, lost, or stuck, I commit to going back to re-read this agreement with myself and to say or write: "I'm worthy. I'm perfectly on track. I've got this." I am ready to turn pain into gain and manifest miracles. I'm all in!"

Sincerely,
(Your Name)

How did it feel to sign this agreement with yourself? Now that you've gone *all in* on your desires, life can too. Latent forces are being mobilized by Spirit on your behalf to support you in unimaginable ways! Your life will never be the same. You will never be the same. Let's get started!

4:

Assess Your Life

"When you change the way you look at things, the things you look at change."

—Wayne Dyer

Awareness is a one-way door. Once you know, you can't un-know. So many of us spend so much of our lives running away from our insecurities, fears, pain, and even our desires, gifts, and dreams. Unfortunately, denying, burying, or ignoring resistance does not make it disappear. It only makes it feel bigger and more powerful than you.

The tough part of raising awareness is that you can't just increase the volume selectively. You will see where you have unresolved pain, hidden trauma, and painful resistance. You will also see where you have untapped talents, hidden potential, and painfully strong desires. You will start seeing your potential and opportunities more clearly, and you will also start to see where you are stuck or limited more lucidly.

I'm here to remind you that this is a great thing because by facing and embracing your light and your shadows, you will find your power.

"The wound is the place where the Light enters you," Rumi reminds us. So in order to let in more light – healing, love, empowerment, success – we've got to assess and address the darkness head-on. Once we've processed our pain and fears, we'll process our unfulfilled dreams, which may seem even scarier to some.

As Marianne Williamson said so wisely, "Our deepest fear is not that we are inadequate. Our deepest fear is that we are powerful beyond measure. It is our light, not our darkness that most frightens us. We ask ourselves, 'Who am I to be brilliant, gorgeous, talented, fabulous?' Actually, who are you not to be?"

In this chapter, we will face ourselves: our glitter and our gremlins, our gifts and our guts. Not because we want to stir up discomfort, but because the only way to win is to stop fighting and to see your foe as your friend. We want to become more available to hearing all of our emotions to guide us on our path of self-realization and miracle-making.

I encourage you to trust the process and just do everything one step at a time.

Playing the Full Keyboard

The analogy I like to use for mindset work is that the way you train the mind is very similar to the way that you would train the body. If you want to get more healthy or fit and feel better in your body, you can't just do one thing.

Just like with physical training, it isn't just about lifting weights to build strength, or doing only plyometrics or drills to develop more power and agility, or just doing cardio to get lean and increase stamina. It's about doing all of these exercises because they are all integral to creating a stronger, more agile, powerful, healthy, and fit body.

Same with diet – you can't create optimum health and vitality in the body by just focusing on one thing. You will need at least three different areas of focus: what you take in (water, food, nutrients), how much gets absorbed (this is key to actually seeing the benefit), and what gets excreted (also vital for health).

So I'd love to give you a similar analogy for the Miracle Mindset. Let's imagine that we could divide all possible human emotions into a scale. Imagine piano keys with different octaves. Let's divide this imaginary keyboard into three sections: the lower range of tones are "negative" emotions, the middle range are "neutral" emotions, and the higher set of tones are "positive" emotions.

Lower tones are what most people call negative, or strong painful emotions such as:

- Powerlessness/Fear
- Grief/Depression
- Shame/Blame
- Revenge/Jealousy
- Anger/Hatred
- Frustration/Anxiety
- Pessimism/Doomsday

Middle tones are any emotions that have a slightly positive or slightly negative aspect, but are largely what most people accept as "normal" to feel throughout the day:

- Doubt/Worry
- Disappointment/Overwhelm
- Bored/ Lost
- Neutral/Numb
- Realistic/Hopeful

Higher tones are what most people call positive, or strong joyful emotions such as:

- Joy/Happiness
- Freedom/Carefree
- Love/Adoration
- Fulfillment/Satisfaction
- Passion/Purpose
- Optimism/Inspiration

As any musician or singer will tell you, in order to become masterful, you will need to be able to play the full spectrum of notes. No note is inherently better than another—it's the combination of all the sounds that creates masterpieces.

So in the coming chapters, we will approach developing the Miracle Mindset from three different perspectives:

1. Working with the lower end of emotions – we will learn to embrace shadows, resistance, and challenges as a beautiful part of the process. This is equivalent to doing weight training so you can lift heavier and heavier weights to feel stronger.

2. Working with the middle tier of emotions – we will learn how to make the ordinary feel extraordinary. This is equivalent to doing cardio training and developing

stamina and endurance. It's the skill of finding the joy, alignment, appreciation, and awe in the daily grind and frequent ups and downs of life.

3. Working with the higher end of emotions – we will expand our capacity to see new possibilities, think more clearly, receive more support, and feel more inspired and guided. This is equivalent to doing plyometrics or drills – the quick bursts of movement develop more power and agility so you can go higher and faster and be at the top of your game.

Most of this chapter we will be focused on working with the lower and higher emotions. This will give you a better understanding of how you may have been escaping or denying some of them and that's what has made you feel stuck or limited at times. This stickiness is what is preventing you from receiving the miracles you are asking for.

Then in future chapters we will be addressing the middle tier – the place you must usually move through in order to get from lower to higher tones, and vice versa. That's the bridge that allows you to travel freely from one emotion to another and be able to feel like you're the master of your mind—not a slave to it.

Start at the Beginning

A quick note before we begin the exercises in this chapter: if strong emotions come up, take a deep breath, walk away for a bit, or go back and re-read the agreement you signed in Chapter 3 to see this through as an experiment. I promise this experience won't kill you. It will do just the opposite – give you a new lease on life!

The self-awareness work we will be doing in this chapter is all about identifying your goals at their basic emotional state – your core desired feelings. Once you can determine the essence of what you crave – what you need to feel complete and what you desire more than anything – then you can identify the very foundation of the big miracles you desire.

You only want those specific manifestations because you think they will make you feel a certain way. For example, most people want a partner because they believe they will then feel loved, seen, understood, and supported. One of my clients, Cece, was at the brink of a divorce with her husband. They had been married for eight years and had drifted apart, according to her. She felt like he stopped caring, and that he preferred to travel and be with his friends rather than spend time with her. They hardly had anything in common anymore and it was so painful for her to admit that maybe they were just over.

While in my program, she began seeing the ways she was unconsciously pushing her husband away with her constant resentment of how he doesn't love her enough. She realized that so much of her focus was on *him* to meet her needs that she'd neglected meeting her own. In one coaching call, we worked on identifying ways she felt loved, seen, valued, supported, and adored. Within a few weeks, she reconnected with old friends, joined a new hiking group, spent more time in nature doing what she loved, and even booked a trip somewhere she'd wanted to go to for a long time with a friend instead of her husband.

Lo and behold, as she stopped obsessing over how her husband wasn't meeting her needs and started focusing on filling her own cup, she felt better. She started feeling vibrant and irresistible. And guess what? All of a sudden her husband was chasing her. He was showing her the kind of attention and affection that she didn't believe was possible.

That's when it hit her: he had tried supporting and loving her for so many years, but she couldn't receive it and would shut it down by reacting, criticizing, and rejecting his attempts at connection. It was like he was knocking, but she couldn't open the door. Now that she had learned how to open it for herself, she could let him in as well. The bonus? She now had *so* many other ways she felt cherished and appreciated besides just in her marriage!

The mastery is in wanting what you've already got so that you can get more of what you want. Like Cece, if you can make peace with and appreciate every part of your life so far, you will be able to freely create what you want in your life going forward. The manifestations may look different than you imagined, but life will never cease to surprise and delight you, and you will recognize it by the way that it feels.

The Miracle Mindset will invite you to connect with your Soul and this magnificent universe in a way that feels intimate and personal. You will feel like this whole existence is for you. You will see that you are a vital, unique, and beautiful part of this universe and that every level and shape of support is available to you when you learn how to call it in and receive it.

The truth is, you can have the essence of what you desire in a million different ways. Most people block thousands of ways they could be experiencing the freedom, abundance, love, and healing they are asking for because they are so narrowly expecting it to only come through one avenue. This is so shortsighted! Do you really believe the power that creates worlds can't send you the manifestations in a gazillion different ways?

Getting the one narrowly defined manifestation you think you need to feel satisfied does not guarantee that you'll actually feel the core desired feeling you are truly after. So, the exercises below are about identifying *why* you want what you want and how to create it in your life *now*.

As you learn how to feel your core desired feelings on command in your miracle practices, this mirror-like reality will begin to instantly reflect it to you in specific ways. All of a sudden, your partner will start giving you what you want, new opportunities for abundance will reveal themselves, you will find amazing new ways of supporting your body to get healthier and better... So many of my clients feel like the waters start parting and the things they've been asking for are flowing in effortlessly!

That's what happens when you truly understand that life is one giant mirror reflecting *you* back to you in endless ways. In this chapter, we'll identify what you've been mirroring unintentionally so you can make sense of why things happened the way they happened in the past. And in future chapters, you will discover how to deliberately turn your frown upside down so the world reflects back to you what you already feel in miraculous ways!

Wheel of Life Exercise

Wheel of Life is a popular coaching tool you can use to take a bird's-eye view of your life and become more aware of the overall balance or lack of it. Awareness is power. Allow yourself to be honest about where you currently are. By the end of this book, you will have made huge progress towards a much more balanced and expanded Wheel of Life!

Instructions

We'll walk through the steps here. But if you go to www.lanash-lafer.com/wheel, you can also download a Wheel of Life worksheet that you can fill out.

Start by taking a blank piece of paper and drawing a large circle. Divide the circle into eight pie-slice sections by drawing four lines across: one vertical, one horizontal, and two diagonal ones. So, you should now have a drawing of a large eight-slice pie.

Now, let's assess each area of your life and how well you feel in it on a scale from zero to ten (with zero being the worst and ten the best). Feel free to use the questions below as guidance when considering each part of your life. You could even rate each of these questions and then take an average of the answers to find your score for each area of the Wheel.

1. Personal Growth
    - How worthy and deserving do you feel?
    - How much do you trust in your ability to deliberately direct your life?
    - Do you feel that you are investing in your spiritual and personal development in a way that feels satisfying and expansive?

2. Partner and Romance
    - How satisfied are you with your current relationship status?

- How supported, seen, accepted, and adored do you feel?
- How open are you to more love and intimacy?

3. Friends and Family
   - How nourished, supported, and loved do you feel by those closest to you?
   - How accepted do you feel by your friends and family?
   - How much do you accept who they are and what they bring to your life?

4. Career
   - Are your career and professional accomplishments where you would like them to be?
   - How valued do you feel in your place of employment?
   - How close do you feel to your true purpose and inspiration?

5. Finances
   - How abundant and prosperous do you feel day to day?
   - How well do you manage your finances?
   - How easily do you set and attain financial goals?

6. Health
   - How vibrant, energetic, strong, and healthy does your body feel?
   - Do you get an optimal amount of sleep and rest?
   - How do you feel about your diet and exercise?

7. Physical Environment
   - How comfortable, safe, and satisfied do you feel in your home?

- How much do you love the area you live in?
- How inspiring is the environment around you?

8. Fun and Recreation
   - How much do you value having fun in your life?
   - How much enjoyment and pleasure do you experience daily?
   - Do you allow time to pursue hobbies and things that interest and energize you?

Once you know the number for each area, you can draw a line corresponding to that number across each "pie piece" of the Wheel and then shade it in (zero would be an empty pie piece, and ten would be a slice completely shaded in). That way, you'll be able to see how full or balanced your Wheel of Life is and assess where you have room to improve from a bird's-eye view of your current state of affairs.

How did it feel to do this exercise? Are you surprised at the results? What areas are you proud of and what areas would you like to improve?

Take your time to grieve if anything is out of balance and celebrate what is working. Recognize that this is only a starting point and that in the upcoming chapters, we will do the inner work that will lead to a massive improvement in the various areas of your Wheel. When you know your priorities clearly, you'll know how to align with them. That's what creates that strong and steady foundation for a fulfilling life full of miracles!

Formative Life Experiences

All of us are looking at life through colored glasses. Some people have rose-colored specs; others have gray, blue, or another color. These glasses determine how we see ourselves and everything that happens in our life. The beliefs, ideas, habits, and goals that create these colored glasses were imprinted onto us through the formative experiences we have had in our life.

The deepest formative experiences stem from childhood, because at that time, that's all we knew and we didn't have much choice. As we establish certain belief systems, behaviors, and perspectives, we become prisoners in the version of reality that we think we see. We assume that others see things the same way as we do—that they are wearing the same colored glasses.

What most of us don't realize is that we can learn to be more deliberate in the way we look at things, what we focus on, and how we approach ourselves and life. If we change how we see things today, it will transform our memories of the past and completely reshape our future. Assessing your most joyous and most painful life experiences will help you identify your core desired feelings and give you the clarity to manifest what you truly want.

Formative Life Experiences Exercise

In this exercise, we will take a look at the major experiences that have shaped the way you look at life. I will be asking you to reflect on a few powerful, transformative, delicious, and successful experiences in your life, as well as a few challenges and painful experiences that you wouldn't want to experience again.

Then you will look for a theme or a core feeling in each of those experiences.

It's those central feelings, not our rational thoughts, that attract our circumstances and determine how we interpret those experiences. Together, we will explore which key emotions and assumptions have been shaping your perspective.

With this awareness, your beliefs, habits, and past patterns will now become *choices*. In the coming chapters, we will address how to deliberately choose your perspective, and therefore shift your present, past, and future, and deliberately create life experiences you love.

Take your time with this exercise, as it can bring up a lot of memories and emotions. Just remember to embrace what comes up and keep moving forward toward more empowerment and clarity.

Instructions

1. Write down at least three of the most powerful, amazing, and phenomenal experiences of your life. Pick the successes/highlights that felt most personally satisfying. Focus most of the description on how you felt before, during, and after. Summarize each of the amazing formative experiences by listing a few of the core feelings that you felt. A core feeling is a word or a phrase that describes the emotions you felt strongest during the experience.

   Here is an example of one of my amazing experiences:

   I will always remember what it was like to come to the US. We landed in San Francisco and everything felt and looked so different. We moved our whole life across the world and I felt the excitement that my mom and dad were feeling as they dreamed of building a better life for us in America.

I felt so triumphant that we had made it here against all odds! I was so eager to go to school and learn English! My eyes never opened wider than when we went to a supermarket for the first time and saw shelves full of exotic fruit and so many new foods! Everything was so new, delightful, and exciting!

Core Feelings: Excited and in total awe.

2. Now write down three of the most painful and challenging experiences of your life. Focus your description on how you felt before, during, and after the experience. Write down what need was not met and why the experience felt so painful. Summarize each challenging experience by listing the core feelings like you did above. After you've identified the core feeling from each challenging experience, write down the opposite of those core feelings – the desired feelings you would now like to experience. (If you get stuck, try looking up antonyms in a dictionary!)

Don't worry – you will not get stuck in the negative emotions. Now that you know what you never want to live again (the painful experiences), you more clearly know your true desired feelings (the opposite). By the end of this book, you are going to feel like you've faced your biggest fears and that they no longer have a hold on you.

Instead, you will harness these challenging past experiences to serve you in unprecedented ways.

Example of one of my challenging formative experiences:

I remember screaming so loud I was losing my voice and crying so hard I could no longer see through my eyes. I was lying on the floor, hysterical. I don't remember the actual cause of my 'outburst,' but I'm sure it was about something I asked for and didn't get from my parents. My mom told me that I had so many of these kinds of crying fits that my parents didn't know what to do and would just leave me hysterically crying until I calmed down.

I remember feeling so alone. So unwanted. I felt so much inside but couldn't explain. I was maybe five years old and I just felt like I didn't belong in this family. I felt that my dad didn't want to be with my mom and that I was a burden to both of them. But at the time, these feelings weren't conscious and I couldn't explain them. So I'd demand attention and cry, but it only got me to feel more rejected each time.

Core Feelings: Alone, powerless, and rejected.
Desired Feelings: Safe, empowered, and welcome.

After you have written out your key positive and negative formative life experiences and have extracted your feelings from each, reflect on this exercise: How did you feel as you wrote these out? Did anything surprise you? Where did you notice your strongest emotional triggers and hooks were? Did you notice a connection between the desired feelings you learned through the painful experiences and the core feelings in the amazing ones?

That's evidence of your powerful manifesting abilities!

But Isn't the Negative Stuff Bad?

So many who study the law of attraction prefer not to look at anything negative or painful. Many of my clients have asked in the past, "Why would we reflect on something that's been uncomfortable or unwanted?" My answer has always been the same: anything that you bring into light becomes light.

As you assess the core feelings that you experienced in the painful situations, now you more clearly know what you really, really want to experience on the opposite side of it. Unlike on the Wheel of Life where we look at what success may look like from a more rational perspective, the core desired feelings that we identified from this exercise are what you are truly craving to experience. They are your true priorities and keys to fulfillment. All the other ways that you see success are really representations of these core desired feelings.

For example, my client Lina thought what she wanted was to lose thirty pounds of extra weight she'd been carrying for over fifteen years since having kids. She tried so many things and just couldn't take off the pounds. She was divorced and wanted to start dating but didn't feel attractive or sexy.

When she did the Formative Life Experiences exercises and identified two of her core desired feelings as protected and supported, she had a huge a-ha moment. She gained the weight when she started feeling unhappy, unwanted, and unsupported in her marriage. The extra fat was literally there to protect her from the feeling of rejection, uncertainty, and aloneness that she had felt after a very painful childhood abuse experience, and again after her marriage began crumbling.

After some coaching Lina began writing love letters to each pound and each roll of her body, thanking them for providing her the support and protection she craved when she needed it most. This felt so healing to the very core of her. She started honoring her body and taking better care of it instead of punishing it.

She also looked for new ways to feel protected and supported: joining my long-term program so she knew she had around-the-clock encouragement and support, spending more time walking which made her feel nurtured by nature, and moving to a new neighborhood where she felt safer and knew more neighbors.

Can you guess what happened next? The weight just started falling off. She lost the thirty pounds without even trying by tending to the reasons why the weight had showed up in the first place. So we are going to go straight for the foundation – for the essence – of what you want. You will be blown away by the way the universe will begin to bring incredible people, circumstances, and situations to fill in the desired feelings you are inviting. You will also be amazed by the greater peace and lightness you will start to feel as you experience deep forgiveness of yourself and others.

I see forgiveness not as condoning what happened or trying to forget something horrific. Forgiveness is recognizing the gifts in the experience so fully that there is nothing left to forgive. All that is left is the understanding of the contrast and appreciation for the clarity that it brought.

When you acknowledge your light and your shadow, you can own them. When you own your story, it no longer owns you. You can understand the things you've lived and come into acceptance, forgiveness, and maybe even gratitude. As you step into deeper self-recognition and self-love, you will transform hidden resistance, shift your point of attraction, and manifest easily in all areas of your life.

Core Intentions

Take a look at your completed Wheel of Life and identify one main core desired feeling for each area. Look for themes and how these core desired feelings compare to the Formative Life Experience desired feelings. Really tune into each of the desired feelings and notice which ones get you to feel something in your bones. You want to sift out two or three key emotions that really move you and elicit a strong emotional response. The goal by the end of this chapter is to have two or three key words or phrases that describe the very essence of why you want what you want.

For example, when I first did this exercise I noticed such strong feelings of abandonment and feeling not heard or valued that I knew that was something that I would spend the rest of my life looking for. I realized that this concern of being rejected for being me percolated through every area of my life: friendships, school, work, etc. I even felt strong feelings of abandonment when it came to my body. During years of binge eating, I just wanted to crawl out of my skin and leave this awful body that I felt so powerless to feel OK in and make into a size two.

So I knew that a core desired feeling of acceptance was going to be a major key to happiness in my life. It connected the dots for me of why I wanted to be known as an expert, why I wanted money, or even why I wanted a husband and kids – I was craving the feeling of acceptance for who I am that I didn't get in my childhood.

The other key feeling I identified was feeling empowered to choose what I want. I hated feeling limited, stuck, or like there wasn't a way out – it felt so suffocating. So my core intentions for the rest of my life will be *empowered* and *bold*. Any manifestations that will feel satisfying to me will have the essence of feeling powerful, bold, and free to choose what I truly want. Without these emotions, no matter how great the manifestation, I wouldn't actually be happy. With these emotions at the root, the manifestations I create will feel fulfilling and soul-satisfying.

When I focus on how I want to feel – which connects me to Spirit and moves seen and unseen forces in this universe to act on my behalf – I invite the matching manifestations to my emotions to flow in through truly surprising, delightful, and miraculous ways! For example, I stopped expecting my husband to give me the intimacy, acceptance, and empowerment I was craving. I was constantly disappointed that he couldn't treat me the way I wanted and it felt like we were speaking different languages. After focusing on my core intentions, I began to open up to new ways of receiving what I had been asking for.

I began developing much stronger and deeper female relationships where I felt truly received and supported. This was so healing, empowering, and truly miraculous – it literally felt like I was evaporating decades of pain and suffering and creating a brand new framework for relationships. Eventually, this improved my marriage, my work interactions, and even my online presence. It changed my relationship with myself at a foundational level: how I treated myself, the daily inner dialogue I had, and the choices I made. It basically transformed me from the inside out and gave me what I truly, deeply, badly wanted. Had I simply focused on manifesting my husband being different, I doubt I would have actually made much progress.

Do you see the massive value in laying a solid, clear, and focused foundation of your core desires and key intentions?

Identify What You Want Exercise

I will give you one more hint if you seem to be stuck and can't identify what your core intentions are. You can try doing an exercise based on Esther and Jerry Hicks' Do & Don't process. It's super simple and helps you know what you want by focusing on what might be louder in your mind: knowing what you absolutely do not want.

Instructions

Get a piece of paper or open a digital document. Pick an area where you want to see a miracle or where you haven't been able to manifest easily, and write it down at the top. Then draw or add a vertical line dividing the page in two halves. On one side write "What I Want" at the top. On the other side write "What I Don't Want" at the top.

Begin by listing each of the things you don't want to experience on this topic on one side of the paper. Keep going until there is nothing else you can think of. Allow yourself to express every fear, uncertainty, and insecurity. After you've fully expressed what you don't want, write the opposite of each statement on the left-hand side of the page to show what you do want.

So if you wrote on the What I Don't Want side "feel like I'll never figure this out," you can write "have clarity and know the solution to this" on the What I Want side.

After you've finished the exercise, fold the sheet in half. Now tear off the right-hand side and throw it away. Now you have a list of feelings and experiences that you can focus on to manifest those outcomes! As you review this list, look for key themes to extract your top two to three core desired feelings. Get excited that soon you will be experiencing these key intentions in many ways as your new normal!

Daily Miracle Practice

Whatever you focus on, grows. Practice makes progress. Just like you need to eat frequently every day in order to keep up energy, physical health, and vitality, you also need to feed your soul and mind.

A big focus of this book is to give you tools that you can use daily in order to live more happily and deliberately manifest miracles in your life. Establishing a miracle practice will produce powerful inner and outer shifts over time. First, a few suggestions about the daily practice:

- It doesn't have to be in the morning, but for most people it's easier to do the miracle practices when their mind is fresh and unburdened by the experiences of the day.

- Done is better than perfect. One minute of deep breathing is better than none. Two minutes of gratitude said out loud as you're driving to work will create more positive ripples throughout the day than not doing any at all.
- Set aside five to ten minutes, but don't beat yourself up if you skimp on time or skip one day. Just get back in the saddle the following morning!

Developing the habit of consistently and frequently focusing on your core desired feelings in all the various ways I will present at the end of each chapter will bring incredible and permanent shifts into your life. By deliberately activating how you want to feel, you are in essence inviting experiences, people, and situations that will bring forth what you desire. So I hope you're excited to use the miracle practices as shaping tools for your reality and are ready to dive into the first one!

Miracle Practice – Try Gridding

Gridding is a process I first heard about from Abraham Hicks. After practicing it, I'd adjusted it and made it my own. It was so powerful in its simplicity and allowed me to manifest endless miracles with just a few minutes of focusing on core desired feelings by just writing down a few emotional words in the morning.

What I now know after teaching this practice to thousands of clients is that it is a simple way to evoke and amplify your true priorities and invite them into your daily reality. You will see a shift in how you feel during the day pretty instantly after gridding. It's like whatever you felt in your body as you painted with words on paper in the morning shows up in unexpected ways for you by the evening. How incredible is that?

Instructions

1. Write the date in your journal and then draw a big box. Divide it up into little grids so you have twelve or sixteen little boxes to write in.

2. Tune in and search for an emotional word that feels really good and write it down in the first square. You can pick one of your core intentions or anything else that feels good to focus on.

   Note: do not pick your core desired feeling if it feels too big, uncomfortable, or resistant in any way. Pick something in the vicinity of that feeling, but something accessible to you. So if "acceptance" is one of your core desired feelings and you do not feel like you are accepting yourself or others at the moment, start with something like "connection" or even "warm." These words might symbolize how you want to feel when interacting with others when you feel accepted. So remember to start gridding with a word you can actually feel – in your heart, belly, cells – so you can really enter the emotion without resistance.

3. Spend ten to fifteen seconds remembering a time you've felt this in the past or what you imagine it would feel like. So you could remember a time you felt "connection" and really enter that memory until you feel it in your body. Keep focusing on the sensations and emotions that get

evoked – really feel it at a physical level until another word or phrase pops up in your mind.

4. Write down the next feeling in the next square and feel into that word. So you are pausing and staying in the emotion through a memory, fantasy, or physical sensation of that feeling until some other amazing idea, emotion, or memory comes up.

5. The words you choose don't matter – what you feel does. So you may go from "connection" to "enlivened" to "Sandy's Party" as you remember feeling so comfortable being yourself, lit up, and connected that a memory of a party where you felt this way with your friends pops up.

6. What you write down doesn't have to make sense to anyone else; it just needs to feel a certain kind of strong way to you. If you feel an emotional reaction that moves you up the emotional keyboard toward the higher octaves, you know you are doing it right, no matter what you are writing in the grid!

7. Continue to fill in the grid as you continue to find better and better feeling words. The key is to induce a strong positive emotion that increases and grows with each new grid slot.

Take your time to really chew on the words and phrases you write in the grid. Think of gridding as taking yourself on an emotional journey of feeling what you have been wanting to feel for so long. So, you are using your mind to give your body the sensations of the core desired feelings that you have identified as the very essence of the miracles you desire.

8. As you finish gridding, feel free to pick the word that most resonated with you, write it down on a piece of paper, and keep it in your wallet or on your desk that day to remind yourself of how good it is to feel it. It's like a mini-vacation in your mind throughout the day.

Here's an example: Let's say you start with something general like "ease" that represents the effortless abundance that you want to feel when you miraculously manifest what you think you want – a lot of money. Allow yourself to really remember, imagine, and embody this feeling. You may remember a time swinging on a hammock by the beach feeling the ocean breeze. Or you may feel into a sensation of playing and being carefree and light. As long as it feels good to you and resonates at a visceral level, you are doing it right.

After a few moments of living in that memory or fantasy, you'll notice the next feeling arising. Maybe something like "fun," as you start to feel more playful energy flowing through you. So you can write down "fun" on your grid and ask your mind to take you to a place that was the epitome of fun for you. It doesn't matter whether it's a memory or something you conjure up from your imagination – what matters is that it produces an effect in your physical apparatus and you actually feel sensations in your body that represent "ease," "fun," or anything else that you want to experience in your life. Keep going until you fill all the boxes in the grid.

There is no right or wrong way to do this process, whatever feels best is best! You may notice that different emotions appeal to you on different days. Sometimes a feeling of "lightness" or "joy" is most resonant, and other times you may want to feel into words like "safe" and "steady." Sometimes you won't be able to easily access a certain feeling and it will require more concentration to find even one experience of an emotion. Remember to actively move toward any word, phrase, or symbol that moves you in a direction of feeling better and better, even if it doesn't totally make rational sense. Let your right-brain creative side out to play and watch how powerfully it catalyzes shifts in your day.

You may end up with a feeling of "abundant" or "prosperous" at some point in your grid, but it doesn't matter if you actually name your core desired feelings as you practice gridding. What matters is that you are *living* – really experiencing in mind, body, and soul – the emotions that make you feel happier, more fulfilled, more aligned, and more inspired.

Think of this exercise as feeding your soul and giving yourself what you most want emotionally. That's what will shift your perspective and physiology so you begin to experience those desires in your reality!

Gridding is something that gets more and more impactful with practice so try it out for a few days and see if you notice a difference. Do your best to focus on exploration and discovery so you learn to best customize it for you, not just do cookie cutter steps. This practice will only be effective when you feel the effect at a somatic level – when you feel your body, anatomy, biology, and chemistry actually reacting. Explore how what you call forth in your imagination and embody in your physical body ripples out and creates shifts throughout the day.

Gridding only takes a few minutes and you will be amazed at how the grid begins to fill in with matching manifestations! This is what my client Lia raved about a few days after learning about gridding and practicing it "awkwardly" (her words, not mine). She realized two things:

1. She really didn't know how anything felt in her body and it became clear that she spent 99 percent of her day living in a state of "head up," not even aware of her physical self and mostly just living in her mind. So it was weird to put attention on her shoulders, heart, hands, etc. and notice how much sensation she actually had there and how those sensations changed depending on what she focused on in her mind.

2. When she found an emotion that really moved her, it felt like water to a very thirsty person. Lia had a huge breakthrough as she started with the word "safe" and then moved into "supported," "taken care of," and "valued." She told me that she hasn't felt these emotions before because her childhood was so traumatic that these feelings of okay-ness were a luxury. Now that she was able to give them to herself, she couldn't believe how good it felt! She told me: "This is everything! Never again will I feel so miserable and abandon myself the way my family abandoned me. Now I am learning to support and love myself and it is so liberating. I'm fifty-eight years old and this is truly a miracle!"

So you see, awareness of your true priorities and desires at a core level gives you a fighting chance at actually giving yourself what you need most.

The second important part of this Gridding practice is observing what happens throughout your day after you grid. How are people acting differently? What new or unusual things occur? How is something surprising showing up? How are things you've been wanting starting to enter your life in the most creative and unexpected ways?

This is the magic of knowing your core desired feelings and deliberately feeling them – all of a sudden you will start experiencing them more and more throughout your days. That's when you will start to prove to yourself that maybe you've had the key to unlocking your desires all along!

I bet you are curious as to how this helps you actually experience more miracles in the flesh. Surely it can't be that easy to just *wish* for something and experience it in your mind and then have it show up in your hand. Aren't there "hard realities," physical limits, systemic oppression, and internal blocks to overcome? That's what we will be covering in the next chapter!

5:

Allow Your Desires

"Manifesting isn't about making it happen, it's about making it welcome."

—Rev. Michael Bernard Beckwith

Now that you've identified the core desired feelings – the foundation of your desired life – let's get wild and dream big about the ways you'd love these key intentions to manifest in your life! Today I'm asking you to realize that your only limits are the ones you place on yourself. Let's stretch your capacity to play on the higher octaves of the emotional scale by daring to be unreasonable. It's time to cease regurgitating and recreating your past as your present and build a new preferred reality that will become your new normal.

This quote by Edwin Lewis Cole is something I live by: "Reasonable [wo]men adapt to the world around them; unreasonable [wo]men make the world adapt to them. The world is changed by unreasonable [wo]men."

Are you going to be a follower or do you dare to be a leader in your life? Reason is deductive – it can only deduce based on past experiences. Imagination is proactive – it allows you to create what you have not seen. Accomplishing your big goals depends on your ability to use your imagination and to have a vision beyond what you've lived so far. Do you want to be reasonable and adapt to the world you see or do you dare to be unreasonable and create a new world?

So few of us are taught to be visionaries. After all, the entire modern school system was designed to create great factory workers. The current Western educational system is focused on having obedient students who can join the workforce and follow someone's orders. So, most of us did not get to spend our life developing our imagination, experimenting, or honing leadership and visionary skills. That's why it's vital to systematically train your mind to allow more possibilities – to think and dream beyond what you've seen and lived so far.

Visions are the seeds of your future. Plant them today and you will sow them tomorrow. It's time to lift the limits of what you can allow in your life. It's time to be unreasonable and dream bigger than ever before!

WOW Dreams Exercise

I'm about to ask you to make your WOW Dreams list – a bucket list of things that you would love to experience in the next few years or in this lifetime. Since this entire book is about developing the Miracle Mindset, this exercise is something I recommend you do regularly to train your mind to allow more possibilities.

Remember when we were talking about training the body earlier? Just like physical fitness isn't just about lifting weights to build strength, just about doing cardio to increase stamina, or just about plyometrics for speed, but includes all of these training methods to work at different angles, this is also the case with training the mind to develop the capacity to think and dream beyond what you've seen and lived so far.

So let's dive in! Imagine that you could have *anything* you want. If you could order anything from the menu that the universe provided you, what would you choose? This is the time to stretch your mind, dare to be unreasonable, and challenge yourself to find visions and goals that move you emotionally in a powerful way. These dreams don't have to mean anything to anyone else, but they make you *feel* something strong and undeniable. These are the whispers of your soul and the calls of your destiny.

Instructions

1. Write down five of your big goals or dreams. They may be things like getting a promotion, buying a house, getting married, having kids, or traveling somewhere dreamy. These might be some of your more 'realistic' goals that you can imagine could happen in the next few months or years.

2. After you've written these five intentions, stretch yourself a little more. Challenge yourself to think of even bigger, crazier, more amazing, and more unreasonable desires. What are the things that light you up that maybe you haven't even allowed yourself to dream about? Write down

five or more of these WOW dreams. Those are the bucket list items – what you would love to experience someday.

3. You can write as many WOW dreams as you like. Keep writing all the visions that warm your heart, inspire your mind and soul, and make you excited to be alive.

4. When you're done writing your WOW dreams, close your eyes and spend a few minutes imagining how you'd feel when they've all come true. You might envision what it would be like if you wrote that book, married that man, had those babies, and created a life that felt satisfying, joyful, magical, and extraordinary. Now that these visions have arrived, how does it feel? Get in the habit of letting yourself dream and experience this alternate reality as if it's happening now. The more you allow yourself to go there in your imagination, the more you strengthen your magnetic power to attract them into your life!

5. Now look at the WOW dreams and see how they relate to your core desired feelings. If the dream contradicts your core desired feelings, you won't manifest it easily or be happy when you get it because you will be pulling the vision toward you with one hand and pushing it away with the other. So if you're dreaming of being on *Oprah*, but can't even tell your mom what you do for a living because you're afraid of her reaction and one of your core desired feelings is acceptance... then you can dream all you want, but you will be putting up resistance to your own dreams every step of the way. The visions you want to go *all in* on must align with your core intentions.

6. Then take one more step: share these goals and dreams with someone in your life. It can be a close friend or family member or you could post it on your social media (bonus points if you tag me!). Of course it's better if you can find someone supportive and encouraging, but ultimately it's about being able to shout it from the rooftops for anyone to hear.

If you did this exercise correctly, the last step of sharing your innermost desires and hopes with others will feel vulnerable. You may fear that they might think you're crazy, or tell you it's impossible, or won't understand you. That's OK. No one has to believe in your dreams but you. I've heard the saying, "One with God is more powerful than millions without." So you just need you and Source to manifest these dreams as possibilities. No one else matters.

Let's be clear – if you want to be living these visions, you are going to have to own them publicly. Honestly, how do you expect life to deliver them to you if you can't even imagine talking about them? So go ahead and share your WOW goals and dreams with someone and know that it's more about you actually expressing your daring visions than getting support. Because the universal support is already lined up to flood in, darling!

Get in the habit of letting yourself dream and experience this alternate reality as if it's happening now. The more you allow yourself to go there in your imagination, the more you strengthen your magnetic power to attract it into your life!

But Is It Possible?

You just wrote out your big, wild, WOW desires and expressed them. But do you believe they're possible for you?

Most people don't. Most people think that some dreams are possible – the idea that you will eat today is not a big goal for most people, for example. But other dreams, like getting a million dollars, might seem impossible, hard, or far away. So many of us assign levels of difficulty or impossibility to certain manifestations. That's what is keeping those dreams at an arm's length.

It's not that it is inherently more challenging to manifest great health versus an abundance of money versus a dream home. It's the level of improbability that we assign to certain desires that keep them from being our norm.

I've seen this over and over again in my own life and with thousands of people I've worked with. Let's for example take people who effortlessly maintain an ideal body shape and weight and don't have any major health concerns. They don't exercise much or don't worry about what they eat. They just happen to have a belief system that dictates that their body is healthy and they don't have any challenges. They usually operate like that without thinking much about it and generally take their physical bodies for granted. They hear of others experiencing debilitating migraines or chronic back pain or see friends who are overweight, but they just don't see why it's so hard.

For other people, living the way I just described seems like a total impossibility. They may have had health issues from birth. They may have been told they're too thin or too thick from childhood and have struggled with body image. They've spent years and years feeling inadequate, in pain, in resistance, and uncomfortable in their bodies. This is what's normal for them. Uncomplicated health, effortless fitness, radiant vitality, and epic physical well-being seems just about as likely as levitating to them.

I have lived both sides of this equation, so I really know what I'm talking about. My mom didn't like her body when I was growing up and I pretty much look like her. I heard the message throughout my childhood that I was "on the thick side" and that I should watch my weight. This is why, when my life got tough as a teenager, I found myself emotionally eating, starving myself, binge eating, over-exercising, and having body dysmorphia. It started around sixteen and didn't truly end until I got pregnant with my twins, so about a third of my life was spent:

- Hating my body and wishing it was different no matter what size I was.
- Starving myself at times and bingeing at others.
- Obsessing over and having huge anxiety about food and exercise.
- Struggling with intimacy and friendships because I felt ashamed and embarrassed.
- Berating myself for not being able to figure this out.
- Feeling powerless and disgusted with my lack of willpower.
- Feeling jealous of those who didn't feel this way and wondering what was wrong with me.
- Regretting all the mental energy, time, and emotion wasted on worrying about this.
- Wanting a way out of this cycle of pain, but not finding anything that worked.

As long as I believed that the experience of feeling good in my skin, accepting myself, and enjoying life without any concerns about my body was impossible, I kept it at arm's length. But as I practiced the Miracle Mindset exercises that we are doing now, slowly things shifted.

Now my reality is that my body maintains itself no matter what I do or don't do. There are weeks when I exercise three times a week and there are weeks when I just do leisurely walks every few days. There are days I eat a ton of vegetables and there are days when I have ice cream for breakfast and pizza for lunch. Once I recognized that it's not about *what* I do, but about how I *feel* when I do it, my mind was blown.

I realized that it's not about actions, strategies, or behaviors – it's about making sure I am in alignment and following what feels best in the moment. This is the greatest, most foolproof plan for achieving my key intentions, manifesting my WOW goals, *and* enjoying each step on the way there!

In order to align with your desires deliberately, you must believe that what you want is valid and possible for you – at least in some general sense. In order to receive it, you'll need to start to believe that you deserve it. I love the reminder that if it's possible for someone else, why not for you? So if you've heard of or seen examples of someone living what you want – or you can imagine it – then why not try on the assumption that it's possible for you?

When I was in the middle of a raging eating disorder, it seemed totally impossible to even imagine going through a twin pregnancy, loving my body, and returning to better fitness and health than ever afterwards. Or when I was first thinking about starting my business, it seemed crazy to imagine becoming a well-known coach and creating programs with thousands of success stories by just sharing what I love. I had to believe that in some way, shape, or form it's possible and take one step at a time... and before you know it, I was living these miracles.

One of my clients, let's call him Sam, had a stroke and lost a lot of his motor functions, including speech. The doctors told him and his family that he may never walk well again or be able to live on his own. This left Sam feeling hopeless. He'd spend days staring out the window of his hospital room wondering why this happened and feeling depressed and sorry for himself. He was widowed and his sons and extended family didn't know how to support him.

Then one day, he remembered that he had some of my meditations on his phone. He had taken my program the year before, ardently applied the principles, and saw amazing results: he raised the income from his job, healed some core wounding, and opened up to love again. So he started listening to the meditations while in the hospital bed and it began awakening thoughts of "what's possible?" within.

He returned to doing the Miracle Mindset practices and envisioning himself feeling "strong" and "capable" – his new core desired feelings after the stroke. He would practice seeing himself walking, running, and jumping. He cried tears of joy as he imagined hugging his sons while standing on his own. He felt the emotion of what it would be like to share his story of triumphant recovery and inspire others. Then, he began making incredible progress in his physical therapy. The more he focused on what he could do today and how far he could take his abilities, the more he saw miraculous results.

We met one day in person and both cried when he hugged me and told me of his recovery. His speech was still slightly slurred and his walking was cautious. But the gleam in his eyes as he thanked me for showing him that nothing is impossible was truly radiant and infectious. Now, a few years later, he is getting ready to share his story on a bigger stage and inspire others to dare to dream, envision, and act on those impossible desires because they will become your reality before you know it. That's exactly what it will be like for you!

You Already Lived the Impossible

The truth is that, as W. Clement Stone said "Whatever the mind can conceive, it can achieve."

Just like gravity will universally pull an apple, an elephant, or a plane toward the earth, one of the key tenets of the law of attraction is that, like gravity, it does not matter what the object is. The only thing that matters is that you truly believe that you deserve it and that it's feasible. Then the universe *will* deliver it to you through the path of least resistance.

The easiest way to increase your belief in your dreams is to remember all the things you've already achieved that at one point seemed insane, impossible, or totally unlikely. That way you remind yourself just how powerful you are and what you've already accomplished. This will set a great foundation to feeling like you are totally capable of manifesting anything you set your mind to! Let's do an exercise to convince yourself that you've already manifested miracles and you can do it again.

Miracle Maker Exercise

Let's work on convincing yourself that if it excites you, it's a valid desire. And even if a part of you thinks it's crazy, that it's absolutely possible for you to achieve it!

Instructions

Write down at least three successes, miracles, or achievements that you've already lived. Think about how they maybe seemed unlikely or even miraculous at one point. Remember times when you dreamed about something as a child or begged God to help you with something.

Maybe you went to a college that seemed like a long shot or are one of the few people who moved out of the town you grew up in. Maybe you are the first person in your family who started a business or made six figures. Maybe you healed an ailment or survived the loss of a loved one, or overcame some major obstacle. You may now be taking it for granted, but at one point, this was probably a big dream.

Bring those experiences or achievements forward into your consciousness. Imagine what the you from ten or twenty years ago would say about certain successes and accomplishments that you've had. Reflect on what made it possible and what mindset you were in to allow those experiences.

Here's an example:

When I was dating in my teens and early twenties, it seemed totally impossible to be with a partner with whom I felt safe, accepted, desired, unconditionally loved, and cherished. I didn't see examples of great marriages when I was growing up and I basically surrendered to the idea that I was broken and would never be happy in a relationship.

But after doing all the self-work around self-love, healing my childhood wounds, and learning to find my voice (through the Miracle Mindset practices), I realized that no one could give me what I wasn't giving myself. My focus became on being my own most amazing partner.

It was miraculous how all of my other relationships started to improve. It was like the tide that lifted all the boats. Now my marriage is so fulfilling, inspiring, and nourishing that I want to pinch myself. Every day isn't all rainbows and unicorns, but we:

- welcome challenges and transform them into breakthroughs
- connect intimately at a soul level and expand our visions for what's possible
- have the most intense and pleasurable intimate connection.

I admire my husband as an incredible father and partner and feel so honored and cherished by him. This is truly one of the greatest miracles I could ever imagine! At one point, I didn't think I'd see this at all in my lifetime and now I am creating a whole new paradigm for my kids.

By the time you write down two or three miracles you've lived, you will feel like *anything* is possible! This exercise will help remind you over and over that what you imagine can be real. It will train your mind to see the miraculous as possible.

So commit to seeking out more books about someone doing something extraordinary and listening to more podcasts discussing daring deeds and greatness. I promise you all of those people also felt at one point that what they wanted wasn't likely or even possible, and yet they dared to be unreasonable and take steps toward their "impossible dream." Keep reminding yourself that you have already manifested some miracles, so why wouldn't you be able to manifest more in the future?

Hard Labor versus Inspired Action

Now that you've identified your key intentions and your WOW dreams and you might even believe they are feasible, I bet you're dying to make them happen! At this point, you have a choice to make.

Would you rather try to create it all yourself with manual labor?

Or, would you love endless support, guidance, cooperative components, helpful people, divine timing, and all other manner of physical and non-physical assistance to make your dreams reality?

You can choose to make realizing your goals a difficult, arduous, lonely, frustrating, and miserable process, or you can decide right now that you are *open* to support. You can decide that you are worthy and ready to work *with* the power that creates universes to create a new world for *you.*

I don't need you to believe or trust that this is the case. I just want you to test it. Try out the practices in the next four chapters and evaluate the results the way a scientist would determine if results support or reject a hypothesis.

Smart action leverages the law of attraction and has the energy that creates worlds working on your behalf. Smart action is heading in the right direction and hitting the gas when the light is green. Hard action is feeling fear, anxiety, and resistance (red light!) but going forward anyway – don't be surprised if you collide with something!

When you line up the energy of intention and don't rush to "make things happen," you recognize the clear call of Inspired Action – that feeling of clarity when wild horses can't keep you from acting on an idea. Then you don't need anyone's permission, validation, or recognition. You just do what feels like the next natural step (even if the step seems steep). That's when you hear the guidance from Spirit that brings you clarity and solutions, no matter where you find yourself on the emotional scale. So you go from problem to solution and desire to manifestation in no time!

Miracle Practice – Meditate

If you want more miracles, you've got to create the room for them.

You are probably familiar with the word meditation. I use it broadly and frequently refer to meditation as a centering, grounding, or receiving practice. It's the act of slowing down any resistance or unwanted momentum, tuning into divine guidance, and opening up to what's beyond your mind's current capacity to process. Allowing practices like meditation creates the space for miracles to flow in.

Meditating is one of the best ways to prepare yourself to realize your true intentions. We will cover a few types of meditation so that you can explore what resonates with you the most. I will note which practice may be best depending on where you are currently feeling on the emotional scale so you pick the right one.

The practices I'm listing below are self-guided and simple. They can be done anywhere, anytime. I recommend doing five to ten minutes of centering every day to train yourself to go from problem mind to solution mind. But all of these meditations are also effective when done for even one to two minutes.

One of my most popular meditations is the four-minute Ease Meditation. I discovered the need for mini-meditations when I had young kids and couldn't find hardly any time for my Miracle Mindset practices. So I would sometimes do a mini-meditation by taking ten deep breaths while in the bathroom. Or I would listen to the four-minute Ease Meditation while nursing or in between baby naps since even a few minutes of free time was difficult to find. Yet the effect of spending even five minutes pausing all the busy thoughts and constant doings of my life gave me a chance to re-center and realign.

When we learn to stop, drop, and realign, we access the divine!

It's the equivalent of having some food when you've been starving. You feel like you can actually think properly again and everything appears solvable instead of totally and utterly over-whelming. It's like a chiropractic adjustment for your mind that gets things unblocked and circulating – all of a sudden you feel better, the tasks at hand seem more manageable, and there is a sense of empowerment and clarity. That's because you plugged into Source again and are now connected to inspiration.

I encourage you not to worry about how long you do these practices for and just do them. Sixty seconds is better than none. You'll be amazed at how much less anxious, overwhelmed, stressed, or worried you'll feel in even a minute! The longest I recommend you practice these meditations is twenty minutes. Some mindfulness teachers suggest thirty minutes or even an hour a day, but I personally find that this can easily turn into escapism or spiritual bypassing. Spiritual bypassing is a term describing spiritually distracting ourselves from our feelings, but thinking that we are walking a healthy spiritual path. It's a defense mechanism and although it shields us, it also limits us.

My philosophy is this: do five to fifteen minutes of connecting with your soul, the divine, and your key intentions and juicy visions, then go and do the real work of continuing to feel good while in the thick of daily life.

Breath Meditation

Breath meditation is simply the act of becoming aware of the breath. It is very common that when you begin meditating, the mind will wander. With practice, it gets easier and easier to drop in and quiet down quickly and effectively. Using the breath to deliberately center and realign is powerful because it will allow you to focus on your core desired feelings (instead of what's not wanted) any time you experience challenges or contrast. Now that's a superpower!

Breath meditation is best when you are feeling somewhere on the upper register of the emotional scale. It typically won't be as effective with strong negative emotions.

Instructions

1. Sit in a quiet and comfortable place. Set a timer for ten or fifteen minutes.

2. Begin observing the breath. Keep bringing your awareness and thoughts to the inhales, exhales, and the spaces in between, over and over again. The key isn't to be

thoughtless or emotionless – it's to keep coming back to focusing on the breath and connecting to the body.

3. After the timer goes off and you finish, reflect on how you feel now versus before you began, and decide whether you would like to add more short breath meditations to your life to calm the nervous system, balance the emotions, and become more present in your day.

Fire Meditation

Fire meditation is a way to connect to what's happening right here and now and practice strengthening concentration. By looking at a candle or any open flame, you allow yourself to fully drop into the present moment and clear the mind of anything other than right here, right now. Fire is a very powerful element for cleansing and I especially love to do a fire meditation before any big moment.

Fire meditation is very effective when you are in the middle of the emotional scale, when you're not feeling super positive (off the charts happy) or negative (worst moment of your life), but somewhere more average.

Instructions

1. Set aside ten to fifteen minutes for this exercise.

2. Light a candle, start a fire, or find a video of a burning flame.

3. Keep your gaze focused on the flame and any time your attention wanders, bring it back to watching the fire dance.

4. After the timer goes off and you finish the meditation, reflect on how you feel now versus before you began and decide whether you would like to add more fire meditations to your life.

5. Tip: if you ever find yourself hanging out with friends or family around a fireplace or a fire, you could guide everyone through a short fire meditation and then ask them for their intention for this week or month. This can be a great way to introduce your loved ones to manifesting practices!

Mantra Meditation

A mantra is a word or phrase of special significance that is repeated either out loud or silently. This meditation uses a mantra as a way to focus the mind and strengthen the concentration. Sound is vibration and by choosing a certain collection of sounds, you can amplify their vibration within yourself.

Mantra meditation can be specifically useful when your mind feels busy or is filled with a lot of low-vibrating thoughts. If you find yourself on the lower end of the emotional scale feeling intense emotional discomfort, doing a short mantra meditation can help you settle. Repeating your intention in a word or phrase in any language will allow you to drop the resistance and allow you to start moving up the emotional scale to a better feeling state.

Instructions

1. Set aside three to ten minutes for this exercise.

2. Choose a mantra that you'd like to repeat and decide how you are synching it to your breath.

3. Keep repeating the chosen word or phrase until the timer goes off. If you forget to say it in your mind or lose track because other thoughts come in, just gently guide yourself back to silently repeating the mantra.

4. After the timer goes off and you finish the meditation, reflect on how you feel now versus before you began and ways you may want to add more mantra meditations to your life.

5. Tip: if you ever find yourself really emotionally deregulated, super far to the left on the low notes or super far to the right on the high notes of the emotional keyboard, a few minutes of repeating something soothing can do wonders to get you to feel more balanced and able to move more fluidly on the emotional keyboard.

There are endless other types of centering practices such as Mandala Meditations, Movement Meditations, Labyrinth Walks, Pranayama (yogic breath work), and so much more (just google "types of meditation"). I just wanted you to have a basic understanding of the main types of self-guided meditations. In the next chapter, we will dive into guided meditations, also known as visualizations. They are forms of Guided Imagery and frequently used to amplify positive momentum and speed up manifestations!

6:

Imagine the Impossible

*"Use your imagination until your
big dream feels so familiar that the
manifestation is the next logical step."*

— Abraham Hicks

Where you currently stand in your life is a result of your past thoughts and beliefs. Where you go next is determined by your present way of thinking, feeling, and living. Once you become aware of long-term patterns, beliefs, and habits that no longer serve you, you will want to shift them. The question I hear a lot is, "Now that I know what's not working and I know where I want to go, how do I get there?"

Well, the truth is that if you have a train going a hundred miles an hour in one direction, it's going to be really hard to turn it around at that speed. You want to slow down almost to a stop and then turn in the direction you want to go and then add velocity. Then you'll get to a hundred miles per hour in that direction in no time. If meditation, or centering practices, are about slowing down the train heading in the wrong (unwanted) direction and redirecting it in the right (desired) direction, then visioning is all about adding momentum to increase the speed to arrive at your desires faster.

If you are envisioning your nightmares, you will manifest them a lot faster. I am suggesting you learn how to deliberately and consistently vision your dreams, so your core intentions materialize faster! Visioning practices are essential for living in alignment, being receptive to infinite support, and gaining strides toward your goals. Creative Visioning is all about bringing to mind and into your body a felt sense of what you want to be living – something that excites, enlivens, and inspires you.

In the coming chapters, you will discover which visioning tools are most effective and potent for you. The opportunity here is *huge*! You will begin to experience much greater peace, joy, and harmony throughout your days. Isn't that a miracle within itself?

When you are plugged into Source, you will feel like there is endless electricity powering everything you do. You'll feel so energized, inspired, focused, and so darn on purpose that you'll start to have moments of superhuman feats. I once had a client, Alice, tell me that she became so inspired in her life that she started waking up at 5:00 a.m. and getting more done before her kids woke up than she used to do in the whole day! She had time to do her mindset practice, work out, prep lunches, pay bills, and more. Plus, she was able to enjoy leisurely mornings with her kids while getting everyone to school and work on time!

After her morning miracle practice, Alice felt so energized throughout the day that she was able to complete more work than her peers, so she got an unexpected promotion. She was also encouraged to go for further certification and study for it during work hours! As she felt more confident going for what made her happy, she decided to become a Zumba dance instructor. She told me excitedly that she couldn't believe she's getting paid to dance, bring joy, and get more fit! This was a huge dream come true because she used to be a dancer when she was young but had felt out of shape and out of connection with her body for so long. Through the Miracle Mindset, she tapped into endless energy and miraculous support from life so she was able to keep reaching for bigger and bigger dreams!

Before you know it, you'll be able to tirelessly do something that used to exhaust you, you'll feel thrilled and excited when facing challenges that previously defeated you, and you'll spend more and more of your days in gratitude, celebration, and awe. As you step into greater personal alignment, the synchronicities, miracles, and manifestations that follow will truly blow you away!

Guided Imagery Overview

There are four types of visioning that we will cover: Guided Imagery, Written Expression, Spoken Expression, and Creative Expression. This chapter is all about Guided Imagery, also known as creative visualization (or simply visualization).

It's paramount to have a clear, embodied vision of your desire so that you are receptive to all the cooperative components, opportunities, people, and angels that are working on your behalf to bring this vision to life. Creative visualization involves forming mental images that evoke strong physical sensations in order to step into a vibrational space where you become a match to what you are seeking to attract.

There's a lot of scientific research describing how visualization works on the physical level. Turns out your brain can't tell when you are imagining something or when you're actually living it. Your hormones, adrenaline, and other biological markers respond similarly whether you get frightened by a monster in a movie or are facing one in real life. When you're experiencing fear, your body begins preparing for fight or flight, triggering a series of chemical and neurological reactions. When you are evoking feelings of joy, love, and passion, your body reacts as if you are in the arms of a loved one.

For example, when you visualize riding a bike, the same motor neurons fire signals to your brain as if you're actually pedaling. This means your brain will react faster when on the bike next time because your motor memory connections have improved. Moreover, not only did your body and brain gain expertise in what you visualized, but you are now primed for seeing bicycles and bicycle-like movement everywhere. So you may begin to notice more bikes on the street or notice someone who has shapely leg muscles indicative of biking frequently.

This means that your perspective has shifted and you are seeing the world through new eyes. Just as you can train yourself to be a better cyclist (or sniper – athletes and soldiers have used visualization for decades to prepare for extreme physical and psychological conditions), you can also visualize your way to becoming a wealthier, happier, healthier, and more fulfilled version of yourself.

There are two main modes of creative visualization: self-guided and guided by someone else. Let's first explore a way of visualizing with a guide because for most people this offers a structure where they can let go and simply follow instructions, instead of needing to guide themselves.

Guided Visualization

Guided visualization is when someone else leads you through a scripted experience. This can be done in person or through a recording. Listening to a guided visualization is accessible and requires very little effort on your part. You simply let someone else guide you through an imaginary journey as you relax, imagine, and feel.

Most people don't know how to visualize what they want and have a hard time engaging their imaginations in a way that makes their vision seem visceral and real. So putting on a recording of someone guiding you on a journey that will take you to the heart of your desire can be a powerful way to expand your mind to what's possible and get a physical experience of the dream reality. This will fire so many synapses in your mind – and put out such a loud call to gather universal forces to act on your behalf – that the guided visualizations can literally create a bridge to a new point of attraction and an upgraded reality.

There has rarely been a coaching call, workshop, or course that I've facilitated that did not include a guided visualization. I love to tailor each imaginary journey to a particular person, situation, goal, or desire. The results are incredible! I've had many success stories:

- Jocelyn listened to my Attract Your Ideal Mate Visualization daily and after a week, she met her dream partner! They were engaged within six months, married in twelve months, and had a beautiful baby girl shortly after.

- Krysta used my I Am Worthy Guided Meditation before sleeping every night for months and told me with grateful tears one day that it helped her get the courage to leave an abusive marriage, file for divorce, and start a new life where she is finally taking charge of her life and feels more fulfilled and empowered than ever.

- Erin wanted to manifest her dream home while she was living in a crappy apartment. She listened to my Dream Home Visualization daily to visit her ideal house – within a couple of months she found her dream property, miraculously financed it, and moved into a house she didn't even believe was possible for her in this lifetime!

I personally use guided visualizations almost daily to deliberately enter the future reality I want to claim as my own. I love closing my eyes and traveling to the very juiciest moments of my desires. Inevitably after visualizing I will have a new idea, get an email that relates to the visualization, or have some synchronicity happen that indicates to me that my brain got rewired and I'm now heading where I want to be at lightning speed.

Suggestions for Guided Visualizations

There are endless guided meditations on the web – some are free, some are paid. Some are long, some are short. Some will resonate with you and some will annoy you (like finding the voice of the person a bit grating). Here are some suggestions for exploring Guided Imagery:

Choose a Topic That Really Speaks to You
You can find a visualization for almost any topic: decreasing anxiety, improving sleep, attracting money, becoming more confident, having better orgasms, cutting energetic cords, etc. Here are some suggestions for the kinds of guided meditations you will want to find at each section of the emotional scale.

Lower Range of the Scale
When you are deep in pain and negativity, look for guided meditations that bring you relief. Relief may come in the form of expressing pent-up emotions, releasing shame, blame, or anger, or finding comfort that this too shall pass. For example, if you've just had a breakup, you may want to look for a visualization dealing with the end of a relationship instead of going for one that's about attracting your dream mate. Or if you just failed an exam, got rejected at work, or are just feeling like a failure, you may want to look for a recording addressing not feeling good enough.

You may find it helpful to find guided meditations that help you experience your core desired feelings more clearly. People love my "I Am Worthy" meditation because it helps them feel more at peace with who they are and deserving of good. And feeling worthy is the foundation of everything good in our lives!

Middle Range of the Scale
When you are feeling slightly overwhelmed, disappointed, bored, or even hopeful but unfocused, look for guided meditations that

bring you positive energy. In that middle range of the scale, you can really tip either way and either go left to the lower notes or right to the higher ones. Finding a guided recording that focuses on something that makes you feel eager, excited, and optimistic will move your point of attraction in the direction of your desires. So you could just look for a general meditation on health, wealth, business /career success, relationships, etc., or you could find a specific visualization that you can keep returning to for a boost of positive energy and happy feelings.

Higher Range of the Scale

When you are feeling so incredibly good that you want to skip down the sidewalk, I recommend doing a quick assessment as to what you need. Are you feeling so mentally high that you need to ground yourself and get out of the clouds and into your body? Or are you feeling grounded, clear, and focused and want to amplify this amazing peak of clarity and concentration?

If you are feeling the latter, then this is the *best* time to get a visualization that's super specific. Since you are already on the higher end of the scale and are super receptive, you will be open to visioning without much resistance. When I wake up in the morning and I feel grateful, happy, and in love with myself and my life, that's usually when I pull out a visualization about something specific I want to manifest in my life. No resistance means that every moment of that visualization is pure fuel toward the manifestation and it's always amazing how I see insanely fast results after in the exact area I focused on!

However, sometimes I find myself feeling so eager and excited that I start to feel almost manic. I can't seem to feel my body much. I'm so *up* that I need to go *in*. That's the time I usually just listen to music, go work out, or sit by the beach. All of those activities help me balance out the fast-moving positive momentum and avoid the pendulum effect where I swing from super high to super low in a matter of minutes. The guided meditations I recommend for this state are ones that will help you enter your body, connect with your heart, ground your energy to the earth, and establish a feeling of more ease, spaciousness, and centeredness.

Commit to Finishing the Meditation Recording

Sometimes you'll start a guided meditation and all of a sudden remember you need to add this and that to your to-do list or go do that thing... this is your mind doing what it does best – assuring you to stay safely where you are instead of going where you want to go.

This desire to maintain homeostasis is something to appreciate about your mind, but not something you should allow to run you off the path to the new reality. Kind of like how I appreciate my three-year-old's desire to stop and smell every flower and run after every puppy, but it doesn't mean I stop on the way to preschool to do it and then miss the bell. Instead, I celebrate his infectious excitement for plants and animals while redirecting his attention to getting to school in a timely manner.

So you can redirect and remind your mind that this is the time you've dedicated to this visualization and that's what you'll do now. Afterwards, you will be able to apply the same focus and presence to other tasks at hand.

Creating clear boundaries within yourself that allow you to prioritize your true priorities – your core desired feelings – will have many expected and unintended consequences. The biggest one is the feeling of self-respect and pride in taking amazing care of yourself. It will ripple out and magnetize every level of physical and non-physical support to aid you on enjoying your journey to your desired destination!

Self-Guided Visualization

This type of creative visualization does not involve anyone else. You simply decide what you want to visualize, and then close your eyes and travel to it. You could focus on a feeling, such as going to your happy place or imagining feeling safe while cradled by angel wings. Or you can focus on a specific experience, like delivering a killer presentation, receiving a large sum of money, or buying your dream home. You can also visualize being in a particularly meaningful or delightful moment (such as snorkeling or sunbathing at a gorgeous beach) and imagine what you would see, hear, and feel there.

I think of self-guided imagery as the more advanced form of creative visualization for those who are already quite experienced in various visioning techniques. It's kind of like no longer sitting in art class with an instructor who can guide and illustrate various techniques and encourage the students, and instead painting by yourself and exploring the unique ways your art comes through the brush. Self-guided imagery is usually for those who:

- Like to explore things on their own.
- Have a vivid imagination.
- Can really feel something move within them when they enter their mind-movie.

- Feel safe creating self-boundaries, like how long to stay in the visualization and how to navigate various thoughts and emotions that pop up.

Instructions

1. Decide what area of your life you would like to visualize or pick a core desired feeling. Get as general (love, abundance, etc.) or as specific (receiving a raise, starting a dream job, having a romantic evening with a sexy partner, a day at the spa, etc.) as feels good.

2. Sit or lie down in a comfortable place and turn off all distractions. Notice how you feel. Close your eyes, meditate for a few minutes, or just take ten deep, rhythmic, centering breaths.

3. Find the most enjoyable thought or idea about this topic that feels good. Let an image or feeling arise on this topic, as if you are entering a movie where you are already living the reality you desire.

   Begin to notice what your surroundings look and feel like, what you are wearing, who you are with, etc. Sometimes you may need to try a few different scenarios before you select the one that is most pleasing.

   For example, let's say you want to feel more abundant, prosperous, and wealthy. Maybe you imagine yourself standing on the balcony of a gorgeous beach home that you own. As you let this vision flesh out, you begin to notice the colors in the sky, the fresh scents the breeze brings, the sounds that reach your ears, how your skin feels, the exquisite dress you are wearing, etc. Then you may want to try on a few different scenes:

- Your partner walks in with a bottle of champagne, looking as hot as ever, and offers to toast to your success. Notice how you feel. Does it feel resistant to add a partner to the vision? If so, then try scene two.

- An assistant comes in and shows off a case of beautiful clothes or jewelry for you to select. Notice how you feel. Is it too much to have someone in the vision with you or do you feel excited? If it feels too much, then try scene three.

- You walk inside your stunning bathroom to take a bath. The candles are lit, the bottle of wine is on a tray next to the tub, and hypnotic, sensual music is playing. Notice how you feel. Choose any of these scenarios or think of an even more pleasurable and perfect way to feel into the abundance, luxury, and wealth that you want to experience.

4. Stay in this visualization as long as you can. Your visions will change, but do your best to bask in the feelings, sensations, and awareness of the moment. As soon as you aren't feeling enjoyment anymore, or if you notice any resistance come up, slowly come out of the visualization.

5. Now reflect on your self-guided imagery. What was the core feeling or core manifestation that you wanted to visualize? What were the most enjoyable and resonant scenes and feelings when you visualized? Did anything

surprising come up? This is a great way to explore your subconscious and process what you experienced so it becomes conscious.

Suggestions for Self-Guided Visualization

Feel More Than Think

The key for creative imagery to be effective is to *feel* viscerally, more than think mentally. Imagine the smell, taste, touch, sounds, and sensations in that experience. Really move into the senses more than the mind. For most people, that means staying in a moment in time and savoring it instead of running through a whole day of accomplishments.

Don't Worry If You're Doing It "Right"

Some people form full-on movies in their mind, while others don't "see" anything, but smell, hear, and sense. There is no best way to do this exercise or any visioning exercise in this book. At first it may seem challenging to quiet the mind and find a pleasant scene, but with practice, it will get easier and easier and your visualizations will get more and more elaborate.

The key is to explore what works for you. You know it's working when it feels so darn good you want to keep visualizing. If you are finding yourself lost in a delicious, satisfying moment that you want to last forever – bingo! You are now amplifying the vibration of what you want and it's sending a message out to this entire existence that you are ready for more of these sensations.

Miracle Practice – Visualize

You've now explored self-guided and guided creative visualizing. If you find yourself responding well to any of the practices here, add them to your daily miracle practice. You could start with a few minutes of breathing, then some gridding, and then finish off your powerful morning routine with imagining how you want to feel at the end of this week, or anything else you want to visualize and draw into your experience! The important thing is that you try all the practices and note to yourself which ones feel best and why. You don't have to love every item at the buffet, but you won't know if you like them until you try them.

Now let's dive into another form of visioning – Written Expression.

7:

Write the Incredible

"Cherish your visions as they are the children of your soul – the blueprints of your ultimate achievements."

— Napoleon Hill

Imagining scenarios in your head is powerful, but there is something more permanent and solid about writing them down. It's priceless to realize months or years later that they have come true! There are many, many ways to write your way into the life you want. In this chapter, we will explore two methods: affirmations and scripting.

Even if you've heard about affirmations before, show up with a beginner's mind because the majority of people really don't utilize the full power of writing their desires into existence. Many of those who write affirmations actually find a backfiring effect where they sometimes feel worse, as the affirmation reminds them how they are not living what they are saying.

Scripting is also terribly misunderstood and there is so much information out there telling us to "be specific or you won't manifest it," or to make sure you include "every single thing you want in a situation" or you won't get what you want. This is fear mentality at its worst, and total misunderstanding of the law of attraction at its best. Thinking that the universe and the Source energy that enlivens it are so unintelligent or inattentive that unless you spell out every damn thing, it's not going to get it right? Come on now!

I hope this chapter will help you explore writing as a form of communication with your soul, with Spirit, and with your future self in a way that feels expansive, exciting, reverent, and most importantly: *effective*! My goal is to share the written practices with you here in such a clear way that you try them and see instant results. If you truly feel better while you are writing, you will see it in your day in new behaviors in yourself and others.

As with everything in this book, these exercises aren't meant to be theoretical or just a cursory read—they are only effective when they are applied. So explore these exercises as you would explore various vacation destinations, or how you'd research buying a dream car – try on different experiences and notice what resonates, what feels natural to you, and what creates a new perspective through which you can view your life. In other words, use the ideas here to inspire you to customize your desired future!

Before we discuss each practice, here are a few tips to make Written Visioning satisfying, impactful, and effective.

Written Visioning Suggestions

Only Write What Feels Good in Your Heart, Mind, and Soul
Write the kind of phrases and visions that get you to feel something strongly. You want your written visions to get you salivating, turn you on, and make you feel like you are on top of the world. This isn't about repetition of some good-sounding statements or mechanical regurgitation of some prose. Don't write just an OK scenario – write one that opens your heart, expands your mind, brings tears to your eyes, and fills you with gratitude and excitement. Magic can happen in this kind of writing! If you do it well, it will feel so satisfying – like a rolling orgasm – that you really won't be thinking about when it will manifest, you'll just be basking in the joy of the experience.

Write What You Find Somewhat Feasible
I've seen many people write fantastical tales, imagining themselves traveling to different planets and making love to extraterrestrials. Or others who script things that they absolutely do not believe are at all possible. Of course, this completely depends on the person – to a billionaire, writing a vision of buying a new million-dollar yacht feels doable and exciting, but to a cashier at a grocery store, that is so out of the realm of possibilities that it may as well be flying to the moon.

The key to a vision that moves the needle in terms of actual, tangible difference in your reality is one that is a stretch from where you are, but not in a whole other universe. So make sure that what you vision aligns clearly and directly to your core desired intentions. As your core desires change, so will your visions. Just make sure that there is a direct correlation between what you think you want (stuff, manifestations, situations) and how you want to feel (your core desired feelings).

When I first started writing affirmations years ago, I'd write things like, "I'm a billionaire jet-setting the world," "I have three amazing kids and a dog," or, "I adore myself fully." Even though it sounded good on paper, it was nowhere close to where I was currently standing.

I didn't even have $10K to my name or a partner or a single child... why in the world was I trying to jump twenty steps ahead? What I actually wanted to feel was valued, wanted, and on-purpose. So I scaled back and wrote visions and affirmations about feeling safe and secure within myself. I wrote scripts about being so in love with someone that a soul wanted to join us because there was just such a vortex of love and healing that was created in our partnership. And this felt so nourishing! Then, as more of my desires manifested, I'd write more expansive visions. Now writing, "I love my three magical children and my sexy man," "I have a thriving business doing what I love," or, "I'm head over heels deeply, madly in love with myself" feels totally normal because I'm living it every day!

In other words, don't write scenarios that you have a mixed vibration about. Try not to pen what makes you feel both strong excitement but also strong overwhelm or fear. You may think you want a castle, but if you consider who will clean 20,000 square feet and manage the estate with ten toilets and you feel uneasy, then you are giving out a mixed desire. Instead, write scripts that feel feasible and enjoyable. Not realistic necessarily, but possible and highly desirable, even if it's a long time from now.

This is one of the things I work on with clients in my programs – how to be able to actually focus on things in a way that doesn't trigger feelings of danger and discomfort. If you are wanting fame, but start to sweat and panic at the thought of being on stage under bright lights with lots of people staring at you, then you may want to instead visualize pouring your heart out to a small group and really feel that incredible intoxicating energy of connection, flow and inspiration.

When you get comfortable with that emotion of connection, you could start imagining a bigger audience while still maintaining that heart-to-heart and soul-to-soul intimacy. Soon, you'll be able to imagine standing in front of a thousand people and feel the same easeful excitement and deep connection with each person as you share your message. That's when you aren't putting up resistance to your own desires and they will flow in through truly surprising and magical ways. Because you came to an *Inspired Intention* and took *Inspired Action*, you prepared yourself mentally to arrive at the manifestation without cost or sacrifice. That's when you can actually *enjoy* the miracle when it happens.

The Goal Is to *Feel* the Emotion so That It Moves You into Inspired Action

One way you'll know that you've hit a groove with scripting is that it will give you ideas of what steps you can take today to bring this vision to life. So it's not about writing something pretty or poetic, it's about how it moves you into taking inspired steps. All of a sudden, you'll just have to send that text or email, or you'll have a conversation that will lead you to a book or a course for what you *need* in order to get to what you *want*. The vision's purpose is always to get you to feel like you're already "there" and then take action from that space of "there!"

My visioning practices are sometimes hard to finish because the flow of possible steps to take becomes so strong that I want to stop writing and go do that thing. I sometimes call these inspired ideas "downloads." It feels like I suddenly tapped into a new vibration and wild horses can't keep me from doing that thing. My fingers will type ideas that flow faster than the speed of light as I download content for a new video or meditation. As I record the video, make the phone call, or write the email, I feel this sense of wings beneath me, carrying me – it's as if my ancestors and angels are there with me, whispering words in my ears, and I'm feeling so tuned in and in the zone that everything that used to feel difficult now just flows.

These kinds of Inspired Actions that come from lining up the intention usually feel *so* right and so supported that they are satisfying within themselves. There is a feeling of oneness, flow, and endless energy flowing that is so energizing. Then when these Inspired Actions bring unbelievable, miraculous results, that just feels like the cherry on top, because the pleasure came from enjoying the process!

One of the best examples of this comes from a client—let's call her Helen—who was in the middle of a big launch for her marketing program. She was dreading all the things on her to-do list, so we worked at identifying the root of the issue. Before our coaching session, Helen thought she was just over this business and ready to sell it, so she was not excited about doing yet another launch. She was telling me how she was committed to her team and the potential seller, but she didn't want to do this launch and every task felt dreadful and draining.

During the coaching session I helped Helen connect and work with the resistance in her body. That's when she was surprised to discover that she was judging the customers and clients who she was trying to attract. She was used to thinking that these clients were "needy," not willing to step outside of their comfort zone, and that they would be energy vampires. Helen felt like they wouldn't appreciate what she was doing and it would be a waste of her energy and time.

Can you guess where this feeling stemmed from? You guessed it – her formative childhood experiences where no matter what she did, she felt taken for granted. This triggered the feeling of fear about extending herself for those who ultimately did not see, value, or appreciate her.

I suggested that she spend some time imagining her new ideal client – the one she would love to work with – and then writing a letter from this ideal customer to her. I asked Helen to envision this dream participant receiving massive value from the training provided during her launch, purchasing the program, and seeing unbelievable, miraculous, epic results. Helen decided to stop focusing on all the money she'd collect when she sold her company, and instead concentrate on really connecting with her ideal client who has been praying for someone like Helen and her program.

When Helen imagined someone who she actually wanted to support, she stepped into the feeling of how her marketing program would completely change someone's life. Then she wrote a letter that this ideal client would write, thanking Helen profusely for how her life totally transformed as a result of this program. Helen told me this letter exercise changed *everything* for her. She cried tears of appreciation for her ability to impact so many ideal clients in such a powerful way. As Helen changed her perspective, her whole experience changed.

All of a sudden, she got inspired download after download of videos, emails, and posts her team could do to better support the ideal clients during the launch. It felt effortless and fun. She had the most successful launch in the history of the company, and the best part is that it felt so enjoyable to Helen and her team, like they were truly serving from a place of inspiration and creating massive impact in people's lives, which was why Helen started her company in the first place!

She used the vision of her ideal customer writing to her to connect her to the very essence of her desire. It took her right to the heart of her core intentions of feeling safe, valued, and truly on purpose. The flurry of action that this mindset shift inspired in her is what created an epic experience with miraculous results. Had Helen kept trying to write the same old tired visions of how great it would feel to sell the company and how this launch would be finally over... she would have continued to take hard, resistant, drag-your-feet action steps that would have left her feeling miserable *no matter the result*.

After she refocused her miracle practice on something that was aligned with her core intentions and felt inspiring and resonant, she became unstoppable. Brilliant ideas flowed in, endless energy coursed through her veins to implement those ideas, and she felt like she was carried by life to co-create the kind of experience that was a win/win for everyone involved. And within six months of this magnificent launch, Helen sold her company for close to a million dollars. That's the power of writing visions from a place of aligned intentions that leads to miraculous results!

Affirmations

An affirmation is a statement of declaring an assertion. It's proclaiming something to be true. It's typically a statement or phrase that you aspire to create in your life. Ideally, the statement is in present tense, in first person point of view, and is succinct.

So between, "We finally have enough money to pay for rent and my bills without needing to ask for an extension or worrying about getting the electricity shut off" and, "I am abundant and supported in every way," the second one is better. But to make it even stronger, you could make it more specific: "I am receiving money in expected and miraculous ways! It feels so good to take care of my monthly expenses and watch my savings grow!"

They key is to always – say it with me! – *feel* good as you are writing affirmations. That means you get little butterflies in your stomach or feel a warm wave of pleasure wash over you. Or maybe it makes you smile or chuckle. As long as you feel an emotional response to what you are writing, it is paving new neural pathways and shifting your point of attraction to become your new reality!

Ways to Use Affirmations

Affirm How You Want to Feel

You can amplify and add momentum to your core desired feelings by turning them into simple written affirmations. For example:

"I feel safe."
"I am worthy."
"I am so loved and adored."

You can also get a little fancy and add some specifics and pizzazz:

> "No matter where I go, I feel secure, confident, and safe."
> "I am unconditionally worthy simply because I exist."
> "I am surrounded by people who love, respect, and value me and I adore them back."

You can play around with affirmations and write things you've experienced before or have seen someone live, or what you imagine it would feel like to experience them. This will, in essence, take you to the time-space reality where this is already the case and you will now embody the physiology, chemistry, perspective, and attitude of someone for whom this is already the norm. This travel into your future self will create a bridge between where you are and where you are heading. The more bricks you lay on this bridge, the sturdier, easier, and faster you'll cross into your preferred reality!

Affirm How Good You've Already Felt
Since the brain is actually terrible at identifying whether something is happening now or if you're remembering something that happened before, you can really put your memory to some good use. Remember the times:

- Someone gave you a tremendous compliment or praise
- You made a huge difference in someone's life
- Someone made a huge impact in your life
- You had a huge success or hit a big milestone
- You experienced a breakthrough or transformation
- You felt absolutely amazing

You can spend the rest of your life milking and reliving these wonderful experiences and, as a result, manifesting more of them. So, you could remember those moments, go back to those feelings, and write down how it felt:

> "I am such a rock star!"
> "I feel on top of the world."
> "My heart feels so big and there is so much love that I might explode."
> "I've never had this much fun, laughed so hard, and felt so happy!"

I dare you to go back to an awesome memory, write down how you were feeling then and what you were thinking, and not start to feel it in your bones again today! That's the power of your mind – you can instantly feel better on command without changing anything else other than what you are focusing on!

Progressive Affirmations

You could go from feeling powerless or ashamed on the lower range of the emotional scale all the way to feeling hopeful or grateful on the higher octaves simply by writing a series of accelerating affirmations. All you do is pick progressively better and better feeling statements.

For example, let's say you are having a crappy day. Your boss dumped tedious work on you, you have a headache, and your mother is pressuring you to go to a dinner with her and you're not sure you want to go. You feel mad, tired, achy, and disappointed. Here is how you can use progressive affirmations to release resistance, feel better, and make a decision about whether to go to dinner:

I'm having a crappy day, but now it's 5:00 p.m. and I am glad to leave work.

I really enjoyed the salad I had for lunch today – it was so flavorful.

I love that I get to decide when I take lunch and have freedom in my schedule.

I love my coworkers, who are always so thoughtful and helpful.

I love that I have a set schedule and get to leave at the same time each day to do whatever I want!

I am so grateful for the paycheck I get every two weeks and all the paid vacation and sick days that I get!

I loved getting my paycheck while I was on vacation last month – I got paid to travel!

The trip to New York was so epic! I loved every minute of the Broadway shows! And the food – I'm salivating right now just remembering it!

I love Thai food so much! Green papaya salad and chicken panang – yum!

I deserve to feel good! I deserve to take care of myself!

I'm going to suggest Thai food for dinner tonight with Mom and I'll order so much I'll have leftovers tomorrow!

If my mom brings up stuff I don't want to talk about, I will switch the conversation to the awesome trip to New York and how much fun I had.

I feel so much better! I am getting so good at letting nothing get me down. I'm invincible!

Some of these statements are more descriptive than affirming, but all of them were deliberately chosen by progressively looking for a better feeling thought. Now you can try it. Start with where you are and write five to ten statements that focus on the best possible feeling you can find in the moment. As you focus on what's working, what you're grateful for, and what inspires or delights you, you will easily float up the emotional scale!

Affirmations don't always have to be grand proclamations – they can simply be statements you write down that help you feel better. That's how you learn you can play any notes of the emotional keyboard and move from octave to octave with ease!

Scripting

Scripting is a powerful tool to make your vision more concrete. It's one thing to see your wish in your mind, and another thing to see it in ink. It creates a permanent, revisit-able, tangible representation of your desire and that makes it feel more real. It's also super fun to find your old visions and see how they've manifested!

I first learned about scripting from books by Shakti Gawain and Esther and Jerry Hicks. I've explored Written Visioning a lot over the years and I hope you will use the ideas I present here as a starting point to help you discover your favorite ways to script the life you want to live.

Scripting is basically stringing affirmations together and fleshing them out to create a coherent story that paints a picture greater than each individual idea. The exercises below are intended to help you imagine and enter a parallel world where you are telling a story of the way things have spectacularly worked out for you. Like any good story, the scripting exercises may have an arc – you overcame all obstacles and slayed the dragon. You are the hero(ine) of this tale, and you are as powerful, brilliant, and happy as you can allow yourself to be!

My Ideal Day Exercise

1. After centering for a few deep breaths, ask yourself, "What does the most ideal day I can imagine look and feel like?"

2. Write visceral, juicy, emotional descriptions. Instead of, "I wake up on vacation," write, "I love waking up on one of the most beautiful islands on this entire planet with a view of the stunning ocean – pinch me!"

3. Go into as much detail as feels right to you about where you are, what you look like, who you're with, and what you do, but keep focusing on how all of these experiences make you feel.

4. At the end of the vision, try writing a note from your future self to your current self, such as, "Wow, I love knowing that the whole journey from where I was years ago to where I am now has been so enjoyable!" This will remind you to bask in and appreciate each step of the journey as its own arrival.

Take this script as an example:

I wake up to the sound of the waves. It's before daybreak and as I open my eyes, the room looks like it is in a mystical, magical glow. As I bask in my bed, feeling its warmth and softness, I cuddle up closer to my husband and bask in bliss for a few minutes.

As I float to the bathroom, I catch a reflection of a beautiful, radiant woman with wild hair and rosy cheeks. Her eyes are afire and her skin is smooth and dewy, in a short white nightie that perfectly shows off her feminine curves. That's me! I am so beautiful.

I brew an espresso and walk out on our balcony to enjoy the ocean view. I feel like I am a queen appreciating her kingdom. After an ecstatic meditation and yoga practice in the Om room, I open my journal and vision after vision pours out of me, blowing my mind and bringing me such pleasure. The amazing life that I am living now is only the beginning of what's to come!

I spend the morning getting the kids ready for school (oozing love from every cell of my being) and passionately kissing my husband goodbye. He is so hot he makes me want to drop what I'm doing and get lost in him. We'll save that for tonight!

As I sit at my desk overlooking the garden, I take a few deep breaths and words stream out onto the keyboard. It's so easy for me to write blog posts, articles, and books! My first book will be coming out soon and I'm already almost done with the second one! Later, I meet my friend for tea, sisterhood, and giggles and I can hardly believe that I have such brilliant, inspiring, generous women in my life – what a gift!

After a ridiculously fun night out with friends, my husband and I get back to our home and make love on our bedroom balcony – best sex ever! When I lie down in bed, feeling satisfied and tired, I remember the wonderful journey to where I am now and how much I've learned to trust and allow in the last few years. I feel so proud of myself. I fall asleep grateful for my life and eagerly awaiting more magic tomorrow.

You can read the vision daily or weekly, or you can script a new vision every time you're inspired, even if it's similar to one you recently wrote. I love to write the visions in my journal so I can read over old entries, and make notes in the margins with dates when the desires I imagined actually manifested!

Please keep in mind that the example I wrote does not have to look or feel anything like what you write. This is the challenge of giving an illustration to something – I don't want it to limit your imagination. Instead, I hope it inspires you to create something that is custom-tailored for you. Write a script that feels so incredibly magnificent, magical, and inspiring that you can't wait to read it again and again!

The best written visions feel like they are quenching a thirst in you and you are drinking up the nectar of your dreams so it feels real, vivid, and visceral. They transform how you view yourself and what's possible for you right here and right now. That's when you know you are entering a new paradigm and are bringing your desired future to the present! That's when you tap into the energy that creates worlds and receive the kind of divine assistance that parts waters and creates windows and doors where you previously only saw walls.

My Amazing Future in X Years Exercise

1. After a centering meditation, take a few deep breaths and ask yourself, "What would I like my future to look like in X months or years?"

2. You can choose the number that feels best. Sometimes choosing six months or a year will prompt some resistance because it feels too soon, and picking ten or twenty years feels too far. Pick a timeframe that feels exciting and daring, but feasible.

3. Imagine where you may be and begin to write out any pleasant aspects of your surroundings, the people you may be with, what you look like, etc. Most importantly, focus on describing how it feels to be in this reality.

4. Let your imagination run wild, but remember to focus on the emotions and sensations of a moment in time more than listing accomplishments.

Here's an example:

Our family vacation is off to such an amazing start! Chartering this gorgeous luxury boat to cruise around the Caribbean was such a great idea. We get to do everything on our own time and enjoy total flexibility wherever we go. St. Barth's was amazing and now we are docked at St. Martin on the French side. It's so peaceful and quiet. All I hear are the seagulls. The breeze feels so refreshing. I love the salty smell of ocean air – it's like the greatest perfume in the world! As I'm sitting at the edge of the boat looking at the water, I'm just so in awe of where I am in my life, I could cry with gratitude.

Francis and I visited St. Martin when we first started dating. We were then both working as success coaches, barely making any money, before grad school, before kids. Look at how far we've come! Francis now runs his own real estate business. He is truly living his dream of doing what he loves and supporting others to do what they love! He is so confident and playful, now more than ever! I love seeing his business soar! My heart just explodes with joy to see his success.

Who knew that my online courses and first book would blow up like crazy and I would impact millions and receive millions? How does it get better than this? How does it get better than loving and uplifting for a living? How does it get better than having total freedom to choose every aspect of my life? I don't know how, but I know that the better it gets, the better it gets! Can't wait to see what adventures and miracles await us in the near future!

As you can see in this example, I focused on a moment in time – sitting on a boat, feeling the breeze on my face, and feeling so proud and grateful for my life. I've written hundreds, maybe thousands of different scripts, and I love doing this exercise because it's like trying on a certain reality and seeing how much I like it, like dress shopping – just because it looks great on a mannequin, doesn't mean I'll love it. So frequently writing visions is an opportunity to work out the kinks and zero in on what I truly want now.

It could be different than what I wanted last year or even last week. Writing various scripts not only helps me get crystal clear on what excites, enlivens, and inspires me the most, but it also projects it out into the universe. The universe is always listening and ready to deliver to you that which you think, believe, feel, and vibrate.

So don't be surprised if many of the visions you think will take years or decades end up manifesting miraculously in record time! I am still blown away by how writing visions of island-themed experiences created a series of unbelievable turns of events and experiences that led us to picking up our family of five and moving to Puerto Rico in 2019. I could write a whole novel that would blow you away with all the pieces that fell together to make this new life of living in paradise, homeschooling our kids, and being location-independent. I honestly sometimes just exclaim in outrageous awe and gratitude, "Who is orchestrating all of this?" or, "How can it possibly get better than this?"

Looking back, I feel such incredible appreciation for all of the years I wrote about feeling safe, happy, and at peace in the ocean in my version of paradise. Because today I am writing this book to you overlooking the most epic view of the Caribbean Sea from our home in Puerto Rico, with my husband and kids talking excitedly downstairs after coming back from surfing on the beach. I just want to pinch myself and scream from the rooftops, "If this is possible for a little girl from Siberia who felt so broken and lost most of her life, anything is possible for anyone!"

Your "impossible" visions, your WOW dreams, and your bold desires will become your reality if you dare to try these practices and learn how to play the emotional keyboard so you know how to use *all* the notes to create the greatest masterpiece you can imagine!

Miracle Practice – Write

I hope by now you're eager to include some form of Written Visioning in your days! You can add affirmations or scripting to your morning practice to clarify and amplify your visions.

Affirmations can be used at any place on the emotional scale and are effective at helping you move up the octaves. Scripting is best to do when you are already feeling generally good and vibing high so you can get better at composing using the higher notes. When you are in a receptive space, you'll access thoughts at higher frequencies and enter new reels of possibility.

Here are a few scripting prompts you could use for your miracle practice:

- How does it feel to have accomplished that big goal?
- Remember when you had that incredible experience?
- What is it like to have the most legendary fill-in-the-blank ever?
- How can this possibly get any better than this?

As a reminder, all of these descriptions and examples are just suggestions. Take them and make your own epic script that feels so good to write that you feel like you're there and living it!

Written Visioning with Others

In the next chapter, we'll really dive into the ways you can co-create with others to step into your desired parallel reality, but here I just want to mention a few fun ways you could brighten up your day by writing to someone:

1. Write a love note or thank you card to someone. You can write a sentence or a whole letter. You can write it by hand or type it and send it via text, email, or post it on social media. There are endless ways you can share appreciation for someone in your life. Not only will it feel good to do it, but the amount of appreciation and love you'll receive back will fill you up with positive energy for days!

2. Share your written progressive affirmations or script with a friend or on social media and ask if others want to play with you and share theirs. In my programs we do these types of posts frequently and it's amazing how celebrating the visions with one another as if they're already here creates massive momentum and manifests miracles!

3. Leave an encouraging message for someone. Have you ever returned to your desk at work or opened a book to find an anonymous note that made your day? It's such a simple act of kindness and yet it can go a long way to create more connection, inspiration, and hope in the world!

One of my clients would keep note cards with encouraging sayings and slip them into homeless people's cups (along with money), into kids' hands, and onto strangers' tables at restaurants. We can't share what we don't have. So when we share love, inspiration, or encouragement, we get to receive it before we give it. It's super simple and super powerful. By uplifting others, we uplift ourselves and become the change we want to see in the world!

Try out the Written Visioning exercises in this chapter and watch how they shift your perspective, uplift your day, and elevate your life!

8:

Speak the Unimaginable

"Your words become your world."

—Nadeem Kazi

Maybe you loved the Guided Imagery and Written Visioning from earlier chapters. Or maybe you struggled with visualization because you can't "see" the images or "hear" the sounds. And maybe you didn't love writing visions because it takes time and can feel difficult if you aren't a writer. For most people, speaking is the easiest, fastest, and most powerful way to embody their desires, but also the scariest and most vulnerable.

Spoken Visioning is the act of saying out loud something you desire that hasn't yet come to be. It's speaking the future into existence. Words have great power. Saying something out loud instantly amplifies and magnifies the impact. How you speak to yourself and to others creates your reality.

For auditory learners – those who need to hear information to learn it – Spoken Visioning is a game-changer because speaking a vision will add so much power and weight to it. It will help clarify the ideas, make them more detailed and objective, and create a bridge to get there.

There are two main ways to practice Spoken Visioning: by yourself or with others. Most people are more comfortable writing by themselves than they are speaking by themselves. When I bring up a simple mirror exercise, saying, "I love you" to your reflection, so many of my clients shudder, as if I've just asked them to give up their firstborn. If that's the case for you, then get excited – this chapter will help you release a huge block that's been preventing you from reaching your goals!

Common Blocks to Speaking Your Dreams out Loud

You'll Jinx It

The idea that you can somehow cast a spell or prevent something from happening by speaking about it seems absurd. At best, it indicates a real discomfort with the idea of that dream. How agonizingly uncomfortable would you be if it actually came to be? At worst, it shows the kind of superstitious and fearful relationship to the universe that will quite literally put a giant closed door between you and your desires.

If you grew up with the saying, "Don't count your chickens before they hatch," I want you to seriously consider whether it's wise to forgo planning, strategy, and forethought about things that you *want* to happen. Maybe a wiser saying to take on as a belief is this one by Lee Bolman: "A vision without a strategy remains an illusion." Or, as Benjamin Franklin reminds us, "By failing to prepare, you are preparing to fail."

The visioning techniques throughout the book aren't about winning God's graces, getting lucky, or somehow tricking the universe into finally giving you what you're been secretly coveting. Visioning is about preparing emotionally, psychologically, and physically so that you are so ready for the manifestation that it becomes your reality. Speaking about what you want out loud to yourself, friends, and others will only amplify, clarify, and speed up your visions becoming your new normal.

You're Being Ridiculous
The other major block to admitting your dreams to yourself or sharing them with others is the fear of being ridiculed or judged. As kids, so many of us were told to "get our head out of the clouds," stop daydreaming, and get to the task at hand. Or maybe you had a childhood like mine, where dreaming too big was looked at as unrealistic, and therefore stupid. I grew up with the idea that if I don't have a clear plan to get there, then it's silly for me to think about it.

The fear of what others may think about our wants and needs runs so deep for so many of us that we frequently suppress those desires in order to stay safe and not rock the boat. We'd rather stay quiet and not even acknowledge our visions than risk being exposed, ridiculed, or rejected.

If you minimize how you feel to appease others or worry more about how you're perceived over following your truth, then I have some bad news for you. You don't deserve your dreams. They won't come near you with a ten-foot pole because of how badly you are treating them. Basically, you are treating your visions as a shameful affair to be kept hidden—not a happy marriage that you proudly show off. How much do you think your visions want to be next to you when you are giving them the cold shoulder?

The good news is that you can change the relationship with your desired reality and start treating it with the respect, honor, reverence, and nobility that it deserves. When you care more about how you feel than what others think, you are there. That takes self-worth and daring to be unreasonable.

The reward is huge. You get to not only be a confident badass and achieve incredible goals, but you will inspire everyone around you who is ready to live full out to go for it themselves.

So you get to decide if you are going to be a follower or a leader, and it begins with doing something new and talking about your goals, aspirations, and dreams out loud – to yourself and to others. It will only be uncomfortable at the beginning – everything is hard before it's easy. You might feel silly talking out loud to yourself, and ridiculous saying your unreasonable visions to others. Keep practicing. Before you know it, you'll be living an epic life full of miracles, dreaming even bigger dreams, and proudly sharing them with anyone around you!

Someone Will Crush It
If you were worried about "jinxing" your desired manifestations by talking about them, then you may also worry that someone can come and crush your dream. So many people worry that others can make or break their dreams coming true. Whether it's parents, partners, bosses, clients, friends... to think that

anyone can take what's yours is ridiculous. It's a manifestation kryptonite, because it gives all your power to someone else.

> *"The most common way people give up their power is by thinking they don't have any."*
>
> —Alice Walker

You achieving your aims cannot be thwarted, prevented, cursed, denied, or somehow crushed by anyone other than you. The world is one giant mirror, always reflecting back to you how you feel about yourself. You either take back your power, realize that you are in charge of your thoughts, words, actions, and destiny, and watch your life align with that truth... or you commit to feeling half-dead, powerless, and miserable for the rest of your life.

You are so free that you can choose bondage. You are so powerful that you can choose to give up your power. But you can also choose to reclaim it.

Frankly, your happiness and fulfillment depend on this and this alone. Because even if you get to the dreams you've had your whole life, you won't be able to fully receive them unless you feel like *you've* made them happen and you *deserve* them. Just look around at the high rate of drug addiction, mental breakdowns, and suicide in highly successful people. That's a symptom of not feeling empowered. All the goals they reached only amplified the feeling of powerlessness.

That's why I'm making such a strong case here that you take charge of your mind and your destiny by deciding that you are the central and most powerful figure in your universe. The exercises below will invite you to claim and own your power. They will free you to go for your big dreams and know that no one else but you needs to approve of them. One who feels clear and empowered is unstoppable and capable of manifesting extraordinary miracles.

Spoken Visioning – Alone

At first, I recommend trying Spoken Visioning alone. It will build the muscle for you to eventually feel comfortable doing it with a partner or a group. Here are some ways to speak your visions into existence and manifest feeling amazing in your everyday life!

Affirmations

We've already discussed affirmations in the previous chapter on writing. Now let's kick it up a few notches and say them out loud. It's one thing to write down: "I'm the happiest I've ever been" or "I got the promotion!" It's a whole other thing to shout it loud and proud.

Try it out – write a simple aspirational statement that you want to be true and then say it out loud a few times. Practice saying it confidently and excitedly. Get your whole body into it. Notice the difference? Not only does saying the affirmation intensify the feeling, but it literally sends powerful sound waves into the world for anyone to hear. Since the universe speaks the language of vibration, your message will be received loud and clear.

Watch how you start to notice synchronicities, winks from the universe, coincidences, and other reflections of your spoken affirmations throughout the day. Just like you are getting instant biofeedback on your thoughts and words in your body – by telling you how good what you are focusing on feels – you are also getting real-time feedback from reality about your shift in perspective and vibration. It's unbelievably fun to have someone say something or do something that you *know* is a direct response to the Spoken Visioning you did earlier.

Get ready to be in awe at the instant, surprising, and magical ways that life will show that it heard you and is already working on your behalf to bring your vision to life!

Mirror Work

After working with thousands of clients over the last ten-plus years, I've seen a clear pattern of why some are able to break through limiting beliefs and patterns while others stay stuck. It all comes down to whether you feel worthy.

You cannot receive what you do not believe you deserve. Today I am asking you to not only declare yourself worthy of miracles, but practice feeling deserving and important!

Self-worth is the foundation of *everything* good in your life. Most people, including myself, grew up with the idea that they need to earn their worth. We were taught that "nothing good can come easy" and that we have to please others to earn their respect and love. There is usually an expectation of struggle and suffering to achieve anything worthwhile. But the truth is, although challenges and learning are a necessary part of life, struggle is optional. That's why some see opportunities where others see hurdles.

Most successful people embrace mistakes and setbacks as lessons, not failures. These "miracle makers" believe that they are deserving, talented, and capable, no matter what their circumstances. Mirror work is a great way to practice feeling deserving and important without needing anyone else to tell you that. The way you speak about yourself is especially important, because it shapes how you see everything. It sets a precedent for how you will allow others to treat you and creates the opening to how much universal assistance you are willing to receive.

Mirror Exercise Instructions

1. Face a mirror, look at yourself, and tell yourself how amazing, special, and lovable you are. Say out loud something like, "I love you. You are beautiful. You deserve to be happy and supported. You are worthy of love."

2. Keep speaking to yourself as long as it produces some sort of a meaningful emotion. Think of things you wish your parents had told you when you were young. Remember beautiful words that friends or lovers told you in the past and say them to yourself. Imagine what you would want your future partner, child, client, or friend to tell you. Say it to yourself and practice receiving it and feeling worthy of it.

It may seem silly at first, but looking at and talking to yourself in an empowering and loving way will help you build a solid foundation of self-worth. That means you will no longer be looking for love, acceptance, and validation in all the wrong places. Once you have a well of love within yourself, you will need it less and less from your external environment. You will be absolutely stunned how this will transform your usual thought habits and relationship patterns and up-level your interactions with others.

You can say any affirmation or phrase out loud to yourself while looking in the mirror. If what you are saying has great meaning for you, it will be an emotional and impactful experience. You can look in the mirror and say, "Life is rigged in my favor," or, "I am an incredible speaker and anyone is lucky to have me on their stage."

My recommendation is that you get playful and flirty. I love to wink at myself in the morning and say, "Hi gorgeous! Ready for an epic day full of miracles?" It not only brightens up my whole day, but it gives me an extra boost of confidence that translates into every action and interaction. It only takes five seconds and it creates a powerful impact!

Some of my clients love mirror work so much that they spend a few minutes every day speaking to themselves in the mirror, knowing that this small act of self-connection will upgrade their whole day and ultimately transform their life. One example is from a program participant named David. He experienced such deep healing through mirror work that he would do it every morning as he brushed his teeth, combed his hair, and got ready.

At first he wasn't used to saying nice things about himself or about his life and certainly not out loud. So he started with simple affirmations such as, "This world is beautiful" and, "I will look for joy everywhere I go today." As he practiced mirror work and got more comfortable, he decided to try saying out loud what he wished his dad said to him when he was alive. Things like, "I'm so proud of you. You are an amazing man." This was so healing because finally he was able to hear and feel what his reserved father never expressed to him in real life.

David had a failed marriage and had gone through a divorce, so it took him numerous tries to be able to confidently say in the mirror what he would want his soulmate to say to him: "You are one of the most incredible, kind, loving people I've ever met and I thank God every day that our paths have crossed. I love you to the moon and back." He told me tearfully how when he looked into his own eyes and said this to himself, a pain he's carried for decades just melted. He's waited his whole life to hear this from someone – who would have thought it would come from his own lips?

The best part was that within weeks of mirror work that got increasingly more playful and fun, David met an incredible woman who was his dream partner. When she said to him, "You are one of the most incredible men I've ever met and I thank God for you every day," he knew that he had manifested this miracle deliberately. Can there be a better feeling than that? This is what's possible when you stop waiting for someone else to give you what you want and you open up to the possibility of giving it to yourself!

You don't have to love or even try every exercise in this book, but I hope you will discover a few that make you feel something you've wanted to experience for a long time. I hope you'll give this gift to yourself and see the almost instant results in your daily interactions... and a whole new trajectory for your life.

Gratitude

Appreciating what you have is the prequel to getting what you want.

Maybe you've done gratitude lists for years, or maybe you feel like you don't have much to appreciate. No matter how awful or awesome your life is, the most important skill you can develop is one of pivoting toward gratitude. Your happiness, your success, your impact on the world... all of it depends on whether you look at the glass as half empty or are grateful that there is something in it.

> *"Be thankful for what you have;*
> *you'll end up having more. If you*
> *concentrate on what you don't have,*
> *you will never have enough."*
>
> —Oprah Winfrey

Many people know they *should* appreciate what they have. Maybe you've done a gratitude journal or said a thank you prayer before dinner. Frequently, this kind of gratitude becomes mechanical, repetitive, and trite. If you don't tap into the exponential amplifying force of appreciation that feels deep and meaningful, you are really missing out on massive inspiration and universal assistance!

As we know from science, our heart also has a brain, and it is an intelligent processing center. When you are able to connect your brain to your heart and really *feel* what you are thinking, you are able to amplify your energy field a thousand-fold. Life responds to your vibration, more than your thoughts, actions, or words. When you feel so grateful, you want to shout it from the rooftops... When you put your back into it and feel it in every cell... You are leveraging the law of attraction to manifest your intentions at lightning speed!

I'm going to suggest a few simple spoken gratitude practices you can try, but remember to get creative and explore any way of expressing appreciation.

Gratitude Walk

One day, I was feeling particularly ready for a change in my life, so instead of listening to music on my morning walk, I began listing all the things that I am grateful for. I tried doing it in my head at first, but the thoughts were jumping all over each other. So I decided, screw it, I'm just going to speak my appreciation out loud, even if I look crazy!

After ten minutes of walking while listing all the things I adore in my life, I felt so freaking good that I decided to make this gratitude walk a frequent practice. For the next few years (and still frequently now), I would walk out my door early in the morning and begin my spoken gratitude. I usually start with something easy like, "I am so grateful that I live in a place where I can enjoy sunshine and warmth year round. I love living so close to the beach! I love all the palm trees swaying in the wind..." I continue to list all the things in my environment that I love, appreciating my incredible friends, recounting something amazing at work, etc.

If I stumble on something that doesn't feel good, I simply go back to an earlier statement that felt great. The goal is to keep the momentum of feeling good moving upward, taking it higher and higher. Some days it's easy to think of a million awesome things, and some days I really stretch to think of five. Either way, I *always* feel better after a gratitude walk – in my body, mind, heart, and soul!

Soon after I began this practice, I began noticing things in my day that felt wonderful. I started taking mental notes so I could mention them in my gratitude walk the next day. Living in this newly found state of appreciation was quite magical! Because I raised my overall inner state, I was having all kinds of awesome manifestations in my life that reflected the shift in me.

I went on to discover many other ways to make gratitude walks even more rewarding. I began appreciating not just the things that already happened, but the situations and manifestations that I wanted to invite into my life. That took the morning spoken gratitude practice to a whole other level! Even when I didn't fully believe what I was saying about my future accomplishments, it felt pretty amazing to state it in present tense and to feel like all those dreams were more possible.

The more grateful I felt, the more I attracted people who felt the same way. Those who frequently complained or judged were phasing out of my life and new friends who felt good about themselves and their lives entered the picture. I felt so much more present, more satisfied, more aware of opportunities, and more in love with life!

How often are you aware of the things you appreciate in your life? Would you like to invite more experiences that have you fall on your knees and kiss the earth in gratitude? Then try this exercise!

Gratitude Walk Instructions

1. **Start out on the right foot.** Upon waking up, say out loud to yourself: "Today is going to be a great day" or "Wherever I go and whatever I do, I'm going to look for joy." This already sets an epic tone for the day.

2. **Walk the talk.** Get outside and begin listing all the things that make your life meaningful, wonderful, and delightful. Don't worry if at first you have to start with something

as general as, "I appreciate having eyes that can see and taste buds that can taste delicious food..." Like any practice, start slow with something easy and then build up momentum. Eventually, you will be able to be grateful even for the challenges in your life because you will know from personal experience that those situations bring the biggest growth and insights to you.

3. **Paint the picture of your future.** If you are feeling particularly awesome, list things that you would like to feel grateful for that are not yet here. For example, this morning I said: "I am so grateful for the amazing home by the beach where my family and I can walk a few steps and jump in to swim any time of day or night." I know that this dream is going to happen a whole lot faster because I am bringing it to my waking reality by imagining it and appreciating the heck out of how good it will feel! This predisposes my conscious and subconscious mind to look for ways to achieve these dreams and sends a clear message to the universe that I am ready!

4. **Gratitude for gratitude.** Close with gratitude for yourself for doing something so wonderful to set the tone for the day. Then go forth and conquer!

Progressive Gratitude

Progressive gratitude is similar to a "rampage of appreciation," a term Abraham Hicks uses to symbolize a rapturous, progressive, emotive expression of gratitude. It's similar to the progressive affirmation exercise from Chapter 7. Although progressive gratitude has simple instructions, it takes practice to get good at it and use it as a fruitful manifesting tool.

In its most basic form, you are simply saying statements of appreciation out loud that progressively feel better and better. You can pick a specific topic or area of life or you can just start with a general intention to give thanks for all that is going well in your life. The key is to make sure you feel better (more expansive, hopeful, clear, inspired, appreciative, etc.) and not just say words or phrases that sound good but have no immediate emotional reward.

Do this when you are already feeling amazing and are on the higher octaves of the emotional keyboard. This way, you are fatiguing your muscles of gratitude to the max and getting stronger in your ability to stay in appreciation for longer periods of time.

Instructions

1. When you are feeling good in your life, name the best-feeling thought. You can say it out loud to yourself or call a friend.

2. Notice and describe how your body feels when you are focused on this idea or vision.

3. Then scan your mind for an even more satisfying thought. Something that amplifies this feeling a few more notches and feels even more amazing. Then do it again and find an even more exciting, enlivening, inspiring, or encouraging thought and say it out loud.

4. Keep going up the emotional scale, getting higher and higher, until you can't think of anything else to say!

For example:

I love cuddling with my kids... They fill my heart with so much joy... I can hardly breathe when I focus on how much I adore them! They remind me that life is meant to be fun and easy... I love how lost we get in playing together... I love how exhilarated I feel after laughing with my whole body, completely blissed out in each other's company! I have so many interactions in my life that feel this flowing, this fun, and this life-giving! I love my life! I love myself! Yes, yes, yes!

Ready to try speaking your gratitude out loud? Whatever we focus on will get bigger and more prominent in our lives. So putting your attention (deliberately, frequently, and vocally) toward what is good in your life is the fastest, most efficient, most direct, and most productive way that you can *up-level* all the areas of your life. Progressive gratitude can be such an exhilarating experience! It's like mental kung fu training to shift your mindset.

When you want to put some focus into a specific area of life you'd love to improve or really enhance and embody a certain core desired feeling, you can try doing Progressive Gratitude with a specific focus.

Progressive Core Desired Intentions

Most people let the circumstances in their lives determine how they feel. If someone is nice to them, they feel good. If someone is mean, they feel bad. You can step out of the cycle of being ping-ponged around by things seemingly out of your control by practicing setting a deliberate intention of how you want to feel.

Focus on a certain area of your life or on a specific feeling, such as confidence or abundance, and begin searching for the most potent ways of describing how it feels to be living your ideal scenario, where this has already manifested. In essence, paint a picture of the embodied experience you desire using words.

Instructions

1. Choose what you want to feel into. If you are feeling anxious, you want to feel relaxed. If you are feeling lost and scared, you want to feel clear and empowered. If bills are piling up and you feel unsafe, then focus on feeling safe and secure.

2. Once you select a feeling of how you want to feel in this situation or area of life, remember the last time you felt this feeling.

3. Begin finding words to describe what that feeling felt like in your body, viscerally and energetically.

4. Try closing your eyes to enter that memory, experiencing the sensations fully as if traveling in time into that moment.

5. Describe what the best parts of that feeling were, and why you love feeling this way.

6. Think thoughts and say phrases out loud that add to, enhance, and amplify this feeling.

7. The more specific words and expressions you find to describe the feeling and visceral sensations, the stronger you will feel the desired core feeling.

8. After a few minutes of doing this, even though *nothing has changed in your life*, you will feel completely different. Now that's powerful!

It takes some practice to gain fluidity in speaking this way, so don't worry if at first you notice big pauses in between sentences or if you can't think of anything to say. Here is an example of when I felt worried that I wouldn't be able to attract the perfect clients for my high-end MasterMind program. I was worried that it was too expensive for some and that there weren't enough people who would see the priceless value of what I was offering. I was concerned about feeling rejected if I invited someone to join and they decided not to. What I wanted to feel was "wanted, confident, and empowered," so here is what I'd say out loud:

> *Ah, I can't wait to wake up the kiddos and have breakfast with them! They are just the most magical beings in the world. Their smiles and infectious laughter make my heart burst in a million little joy bubbles! Our bond is so strong and it's so clear that we chose each other! Feeling chosen feels like such beautiful unhindered flow of energy between my head, heart, and gut. It feels warm, like a blanket of love.*

> *That's how I feel when I'm seeing MasterMind participants on our calls! I feel like we are in a bubble of love-energy that makes us all feel that anything we want is possible! I love the feeling of everyone knowing this is exactly where they are meant to be! I live for those moments when a*

lightbulb goes off for a participant and we both know their life is forever changed! This feels like sunrise in my solar plexus – like a wave of knowing that rises there and moves through my heart and flows out as my words. I feel so close to Source, like I'm being surrounded by light.

I love when the participants tell me that joining this program was the best decision of their lives and that it's worth ten times the money and time they've invested! This feels like fireworks in my heart. I feel this outrageous joy that radiates out of each cell of my body and expands into the world. It's no wonder I sell out of the MasterMind events so fast – everyone wants to be in that kind of energy of deliberate creation and to manifest incredible miracles in their lives!"

One thing that's key with Progressive Core Intentions is that you only do it when you can start out somewhere in the middle or high end of the emotional scale. Notice how I went from something I was already feeling really aligned with (love and connection with my kids) and then built on it to end at something super specific, like love and connection with MasterMind clients.

If I had started with having a sold out MasterMind program right away while I was feeling doubts if I'd fill all the spots, I'd feel insecure, unsure, lacking, and powerless. So instead I started to focus on my kids, where I already felt confident, clear, and like it's a done-deal so I could attract that energy into my life. I can easily move into the sensations of feeling wanted, chosen, and like it's already here with my kids. That feeling is a rising tide that lifts all boats. Once I feel more self-assured, irresistible, and clear, it translates to every area of my life, including my work!

So it's no surprise when the perfect clients chase me after I put out this loud vibrational call.

When you do this exercise, try not to jump too quickly to specifics and instead start in a general place of steady alignment. Stay in each phrase and really discover and enhance how it feels in your physical, emotional, and energetic body. Then slowly move up with each sentence one degree at a time. Eventually, thoughts and words will flow easily, and the experience of stepping into the desired feeling and describing it will feel exhilarating, like it's already happened!

Develop the practice of loudly appreciating what is already here and what you've experienced and you can look forward to inviting much more to celebrate in your life!

Spoken Visioning with Others

Pretty much all of the Written and Spoken Visioning exercises that you've read about so far can be done with a partner or a group. I call this "visioning with miracle buddies." But if you thought speaking to yourself is vulnerable, just wait until you do it with others!

There are more dynamics at play when you see, hear, or sense others' reactions to what you are saying. But those dynamics are also what makes it so powerful! If you can proudly be your glorious, confident, big-dreaming self and share your visions with others, then you will feel like it is done and will be more ready to live it.

Think of doing Spoken Visioning with others as the ninja level. It's something I go deeply into in my MasterMind program, where I give special training to those who want to be matched with a miracle buddy to practice with. This training shows you how to support, encourage, uplift, and propel one another in clarifying and taking Inspired Action on big dreams and goals.

So even though I recommend most people do their miracle practices on their own and get really comfortable and steady with all the forms of visioning first, here are some suggestions for finding the right miracle buddies if you want to try it:

Look for Cheerleaders, Not Devil's Advocates

A great miracle buddy is not someone who is going to judge, challenge, or question you about every little detail of what you are saying. Their role is to listen to the energy behind your words and pick out the most high-vibing, aligned, clear, and empowered moments in what you said and then reflect them back to you. So, an effective miracle buddy will ignore anything that's resistant and instead bring attention to and amplify everything that is in alignment.

If you are considering asking a friend or group of friends to be your miracle buddies, I recommend that you find those who are already aware of the law of attraction, open to manifesting, and enjoy cheering each other on. It doesn't mean you can't share your desires and visions with those who are more skeptical or pessimistic. It just means to be ready to use their questioning, judging, and resistance as a way to get more clear, steady, and empowered so nothing they say sways you from knowing you are on your way to your goals.

Self-Awareness and Emotional Responsibility

In a great miracle buddy relationship, you will go deep and there will be times when you are sharing your most vulnerable thoughts and ideas. So you will want to partner with someone who is aware of their own emotions and can take responsibility for how they feel.

For example, let's say you've been doing Spoken Visioning exercises sharing how it feels to be in your job... and before you know it, you get offered your dream position! You are ecstatic and super excited to phone your miracle buddy and tell her that you did it! You manifested a miracle and this job is everything you want and more! You may even want to take her out to celebrate. But when you actually speak with her, she doesn't seem as excited as you'd hoped. She says a quick congratulations and gets off the phone. That leaves you feeling weird and wondering what's wrong.

This is the time when you both want to have the self-awareness and emotional maturity to have a breakthrough conversation. You could ask what she's feeling and then really listen. She may tell you that seeing you manifest all this success is hard for her because she's still feeling lost, is in debt, and is nowhere near where you are. If she is aware, she will tell you that she is super happy for you and really wants to celebrate, but is just feeling super triggered.

This is a *huge* opportunity for both of you, because you get to hold space for her as she works through the lower notes of the emotional scale and uses the tools in this book to create her masterpiece (she can pick any of the visioning practices for the lower end of the scale and feel instant relief and see quick progress). And you get to do this while maintaining your high notes.

You could do that, for example, by sending her a lovely note with a bouquet of flowers saying that she is the most epic miracle buddy ever and that you are so grateful for her and can't wait to celebrate her miracles with her. Then you can continue rejoicing by taking another friend out to dinner who is over-the-moon excited to celebrate! This will allow both you and your miracle buddy to feel welcome as you are and know you can be on different parts of the emotional keyboard and still support one another. This can be so healing and liberating!

A great miracle buddy relationship can really teach you emotional interdependence that serves both people at any stage of life or any position on the emotional scale!

Strangers Can Be Great Miracle Buddies

Although it's great to develop a close relationship with someone who you can practice Spoken Visioning with and with whom you have a safe place to align, shine, and celebrate, you can easily make anyone your miracle buddy for the day.

You can, for example, tell a store clerk how much you appreciate the lovely service they provided (a mini progressive gratitude exercise!). Or you could meet someone at a party and tell them not only where you've been and what you've done in life, but where you are going (the future you exercise). You could even call up your mother while on a walk and, before she even gets a word in edgewise, you can do a soliloquy of all of the reasons you love her and how grateful you are for her. Watch how that changes the conversation... and maybe even shifts your entire relationship!

Now that you have an idea for who may be a great Spoken Visioning partner, let's dive into some fun exercises you can try together!

Dream Come True Exercise Instructions

1. Think of one desire or vision. Imagine that it's done and you are in the moment right as it happens.

2. Share with your miracle buddy how it feels to be in that space of having achieved this big dream.

3. Describe what you see, where you are, what you're wearing, and who you're with.

4. Let your imagination run free and imagine how you'd want to celebrate and commemorate this moment. Who would you call? What would you say? How would it feel?

5. Continue to stay in that moment as long as you can. When you are done, ask your miracle buddy to share what they saw, felt, and heard when you were in that reality.

6. You may be surprised just how clearly your buddy will be able to describe it and it will feel so much more real since they were there with you!

This exercise is such a gift because the person visioning gets to really step into that desired reality, and the person listening gets to experience it with them! Since all of us are so different, it's incredibly powerful to experience a massive success with someone and see and feel it through their eyes. It's like being able to have multiple minds at once!

It will not only expand what you believe is possible, but give you a visceral feeling of that experience that will amplify your vibration and expand your mind. Now you'll see things differently. When you change your perspective, you change your reality!

I have seen the power of this exercise over and over in my

program, to the point where people literally manifest what they vision at lighting speed and in the most miraculous ways. One example is a client whose dream come true was to travel around the world and have plenty of money to do what she wanted, when she wanted. She did this Spoken Visioning exercise on a MasterMind call with all of us and within six weeks, she miraculously sold her house and got $50,000 more than expected, got invited to go live with a friend in Miami (one of her dream travel locations), and had two clients show up "out of the blue" and hire her! So she was making more money while having less bills and living her dream of globe-trotting as she pleased!

The best part was that all of us in the MasterMind program knew that this was a reality she deliberately created and stepped into while on the calls with us. So none of the miracles were out of the blue—they were out of the Miracle Mindset practices and the Inspired Actions she took! I have seen hundreds more results like this and can promise you that this is possible for anyone who learns to tap into the power of their mind to leverage the law of attraction in manifesting their dreams!

The Future You Exercise

This exercise is simple, but incredibly powerful. It's easier to do with a partner or in a group where everyone is on the same page (and won't think you're crazy!).

1. Agree to speak as if it is one, three, or five years from now.

2. Show up as the future version of yourself and think, talk, and gesture like the ideal version of you.

3. You may describe what you've done, where you've been, and how it felt.

4. Most importantly, focus on how it feels to be this version of you.

5. Let yourself dream *big*. This is all a game, so why not go fantastical? As long as it feels exhilarating, fun, and frisky, dream up anything that inspires you!

This is why my MasterMind groups are so effective – together the participants get to know one another as their future selves and this creates a new identity! When they become the ideal version of themselves and feel truly unstoppable, capable, and ready for what they've been asking for, then cooperative components flow in from every direction. This brings their future reality to the present moment in record speed. From unexpected money and trips, to becoming the expert in their field, or being wooed by the most amazing partner – this exercise, done with a group of miracle makers, will manifest any of the things that you fantasize about in truly unbelievable ways!

That's exactly what I did with my births: I imagined and fantasized out loud with miracle buddies about how I would feel after a home birth with my twins and then I manifested a miraculous birth with my kids born thirty-three hours apart! There were more synchronicities, extraordinary turns of events, and right people at the right time and in the right place that I can recount that showed up in response to the call I put out with my visions. That's when I really knew all these visioning techniques and exercises worked and I had to share them with the world!

"Wouldn't It Be Nice If..." or "Remember When . . ." Game
You can use open-ended statements to expand your mind to new possibilities. You can play a game that not only is fun, but attracts

synergistic components to achieve your desires in the shortest, easiest, and most miraculous way possible. Play this game by speaking a series of statements that begin with, "Wouldn't it be nice if..." or, "Remember when..." and then go into an imaginary way the WOW dream you had came to be realized.

I find that the "Remember when..." game is most powerful when you are at the higher octaves of the emotional scale—when you already feel positive and clear about a certain goal and want to feel into what the journey there might be like. The "Wouldn't it be nice if. . ." game is best when you are either feeling negative or neutral as a way to explore what would feel better to get you out of the rut and into upward momentum.

This game is fun to play over and over, thinking of more and more ways to imagine and retell how what you wanted came to be and was even better than you hoped. Remember to keep it light and enjoy this exercise. If it feels heavy or resistant, try a different topic or just drop it altogether and return to it when you want to daydream and expand your consciousness.

Miracle Practice – Speak Up

These are just a few ways you can speak your visions into existence. Over the years, I've developed dozens more in my arsenal of manifesting tools and have learned when I can use which for optimal results. That's what I encourage you to do: try these exercises and approaches, adapt them to what feels best to you, and keep returning to those that produce the biggest impact in your life.

9:

Create the Miraculous

"The best way to predict the future is to create it."

—Alan Kay

There is one more mode of visioning that I want to introduce you to: Creative Expression. This is a very broad concept about embodying what you want to feel. It's an act of simulating your desired reality so it feels like it's already here.

Unlike Written and Spoken Visioning, where you may still use your rational left brain quite a bit, Creative Expression Visioning is all about giving the intuitive right brain center stage. It's about bringing our subconscious to our consciousness and allowing our primal, intuitive self to lead us to our intentions.

If I'm being quite honest with you, this is the type of visioning that I have personally used more rarely than the others. Even though I'm a creative person, I wouldn't describe myself as artistic. For a long time, I thought that this type of "creative" or "intuitive" world was more for the artists and creatives, not for rational, practical, and strategic people like me. But I've had a few Creative Expression experiences that were absolutely instrumental to reaching the kind of goals that I wasn't even sure how to quantify. I knew they mattered more to me than anything else in this world, but my left brain couldn't even describe them.

Without doing the Marry Yourself Ceremony that I will share with you in this chapter, I know for a fact I would not have been able to create the kind of marriage that I wanted. Heck, I wouldn't be able to have fulfilling, supportive, deeply transformative relationships with anyone in my life. I would certainly be a different mother to my kids. And I'm not sure I'd ever actually finish and publish this book.

Creative Expression Visioning has been paramount in helping me to release self-limits, give myself permission to go for my dreams, be able to discover creative solutions, and take surprising Inspired Action to get there.

Right Brain Versus Left Brain

Out of all the visioning modalities, this is the one that's hardest to instruct, direct, or guide because it is so intrinsically focused on intuition, innovation, and improvisation. With Written or Spoken Visioning, you may find yourself processing information and thinking a lot. The analogy I like to use for Creative Expression is that it's more like love-making. Hopefully you are not filling your head with thoughts about what's coming next and analyzing what's happening, you are just allowing the sensations to take over.

I will offer you a few ways you can begin exploring how to creatively vision. I bet you have already done some of these and can now apply them more deliberately. The key is to find something you enjoy so much that you lose track of time. Give yourself permission to feel like a kid and play!

Let's be clear: it's not what you do, it's how you do it that matters in Creative Expression. If you can be it, you can have it. Creative Expression is a permission slip for you to be the you that you'd love to be. You will know you are doing it well when you actually feel like what you wanted is what you are now having! You will be amazed at the impact it will have on your life – not just in the moment, but in all the moments after.

When you are role-playing what you want, you are actually strengthening the attraction mechanism that will magnetize your desire into your life. It will show up in the form of people giving you the next idea of what to do, books falling on your head that have the solution or some other signs of guidance on next steps. As I've frequently reminded you throughout the book, the goal of all of this Miracle Mindset training is not just to feel better, it's to take Inspired Action and see actual results in your life.

Here are some ways that you can experiment with Creative Expression Visioning to embody your dreams and desires as if they are here.

Music

Tune into what you want to feel right now. Find a song that allows you to fully feel and express that emotion. Hit play. You can close your eyes or dance to really get into the place of feeling it. Remember a time you first heard this song and go to that memory. You can pretend that you are on stage singing this song to thousands of people. Get a brush in lieu of a microphone and sing your heart out. Make this experience as enjoyable as possible – get creative!

Art

You can draw, paint, sculpt, graffiti, sketch, and origami your way into your dream life. Pick up some paints and brushes and do a drawing that expresses your core desired feeling. What would your core intentions of happiness, security, or freedom look like if you painted them?

You can take a painting class that encourages you to intuitively express, or find a coloring book with pictures or mandalas and color it in. Remember how fun coloring books were when you were a child? You can still enjoy them and the meditative state they offer. And you may be surprised how tapping into the right brain will give you brilliant ideas and solutions on things your left brain has been mulling over!

You can also do woodwork, make jewelry, take photographs, or create a vision board or an altar as a way to be thinking, breathing, and expressing the intentions you are inviting into your life. There are endless ways to create art that imitates your desired miraculous life!

Movement

The key for using movement as a tool for manifesting is to move intuitively and without instruction or guidance. Instead, allow your inner guidance to direct you.

Do some yoga from a place of listening to the body. Choose satisfying and enjoyable poses and stretches that allow you to play various notes on the emotional scale. Put on music that makes you feel things as you practice. Light candles or put flowers in front of you so it feels like you are practicing at a high temple in Bali or some other sacred place.

Try free dancing, with or without music. Jump, shake your arms, legs, and hips, and move your body in any way that feels great, releases tension, and shifts your emotional environment! You can also join a Five Rhythms or Qoya dance class, where you are encouraged to release and express your subconscious through dance. It can be very liberating and healing, as well as super fun.

Go for a run, make love, lift weights – move your body in any way that makes you feel even more of what you want to feel. Rejoice in your connection with your body! The key is to let the feeling guide you instead of telling yourself you need to do this and that in order to get to an external result (like losing weight).

Move for the joy of it! You may just be amazed how powerful joy is at overcoming seeming obstacles and paving a way to your deepest desires.

Free Flow Writing

Free flow writing is a way to connect and communicate with your unconscious mind. You can pick a specific topic such as something that's bothering you or something that you want to manifest. You can set a timer for five to ten minutes or decide you'll fill one whole page. You can write with your dominant hand or try writing with your non-dominant one – some people swear by this technique to bring out the subconscious!

Free flow writing is different than Written Visioning in that the focus and the goal is to become aware and *express what's inside of you.* In the Written Visioning chapter, I encouraged you to write about what you want. With this exercise, I'm encouraging you to let go of any agenda except to keep the pen connected to the paper and simply write what comes up.

Start writing without stopping for that entire time. Don't lift the pen until the timer goes off or the page is full. The key is to not think – just keep writing, even if you are repeating the same word over and over or are writing nonsensical things. It's best to write without formatting such as bullet points, paragraphs, or titles. Don't worry about whether what you are writing makes sense or is grammatically correct. The goal is to get in touch with and express thoughts and ideas that are just below the level of your conscious mind, not write a Pulitzer-winning essay.

After you are done, read it over and think about what came up. You may be surprised at what you wrote and it can give you insight into the situation or feel like a release of resistant energy. For example, you may identify a fear you didn't know you had. Now you can hold space for yourself to acknowledge the fear, ask why it's there, and work with it to give you the clarity to go to the next level.

Role-playing

Imagine you are an actor about to play a role, except that role is your ideal life. Tune into the way that future you feels. For example: confident, powerful, wealthy, free, healthy, etc.

You can prepare by:

- Finding clothes that this version of you would wear.

- Changing your body stance or voice to how you would be at that time.

- Getting any props or finding a set where you imagine this scene would take place. For example, you could get a new item of clothing that makes you feel a certain way. I bought a pair of pricey lace-up shoes that made me feel invincible – I felt like I was such a rich, badass vixen wearing them! I literally changed how I felt just by putting them on.

- Make the superwoman stance or sit behind a desk as if you're a mogul. Imagine what it would be like to have incredible power – because you do have it. It's time to activate your fullest potential!

- Potentially get your friends involved in this role-play so you have supporting actors that bring the script to life.

- I once asked my miracle buddies to say a few words they would imagine saying at my book launch party. We were all dressed up with champagne flutes, toasting to the book release while we were on video across the globe, years before this book saw the light of day! This small role-playing exercise has been in the back of my mind the entire time I was writing this book. I saw myself as an expert and an author whose message was impacting millions. I felt the pride for this accomplishment and celebrated with my friends. It's what gave me the fire to finally finish and publish this book!

The sky is the limit for your creativity. Put on your intuitive thinking hat and come up with a really fun and exciting way to experience a glimpse of the life of your dreams!

Test Drive a Car

If you dream of achieving some sort of a milestone and buying your dream car, then why not taste it now? This is a simple way to embody your vision. You could get all dressed up, get in the role of your future self, and go car shopping as if you are already ready to buy your dream ride.

One of my clients did this and it led to some unexpected miracles! An Audi R8 was her dream car, but it was so out of her price range that she thought it would take her ten years to get one. But she went to test drive the car and got lost in the exhilaration of how well it drove, how luxurious it felt, and how nice the car salesman was! It felt so fun!

Then there was an interesting turn of events: someone hit her car (she was fine), she got more money than expected from her insurance, and she saw that there was a deal on an Audi that she wanted. She decided to take the leap and buy it, but was concerned about the extra $200 a month in car payments that she would need to make compared to her previous car. Even though she got all that money for the car from the accident, she wished she could get the Audi for less. She did some visioning practices to feel better and trust in her decision to do what felt abundant.

Two days after she leased the car, she got a call. It was from a luxury car focus group that wanted to pay her $500 for a two-hour interview. She couldn't believe it! She loved the focus group, and they ended up calling her back once a month for another two months in a row for this study! And just when she thought it couldn't get better, she got a small raise at her work that was about $300 a month – more than enough to cover the cost of the dream car she was now driving!

When she told me this story, she said she was so grateful that I had encouraged her to go test drive the car before she was "ready." Now she was up-leveling in so many other areas of her life! This is a great example of how life will go all in on your dreams and bring them to life when you dare to live them!

Rent a Beach House or Take a Vacation

Another way you can transport yourself into your dream life is to go to your dream location for a day or a week and pretend you live there. My husband and I did that for years. We wanted to manifest our dream home, but didn't feel we could afford to lease or buy one. So we would plan two- to three-day getaways where we would rent Airbnbs that were our dream homes or that were in the areas where we wanted to live. Then we'd play house for a few days and try on that reality!

It was not only inspiring, it was also clarifying. That's how we realized that even though we thought our dream was to have a craftsman house in Venice Beach, the reality of living there wasn't our cup of tea. That's also how we "tried out" Puerto Rico. We showed up in the places we thought we might like, not just as vacationers but as potential future locals. Clearly it worked because within nine months of taking a vacation to Puerto Rico, we relocated there permanently! Now I'm writing this to you from my office desk overlooking the aqua-colored Caribbean sea and feeling so grateful that we explored our dreams and manifested so many miracles that got us here!

Besides renting a house they want to live in, clients of mine have also had the following experiences:

- While a client was at a party at a luxury penthouse in New York City, she spoke to the owners about how they liked the neighborhood and the building as a way to really try on the reality of someday living in this dream condo.

- While traveling for work and staying in a five-star hotel, one client decided to bring her regular house robe, slippers, and some personal items on the trip and then pretend this upscale suite was a room in her dream house. She had so much fun doing it and sharing it with other participants in my program! It inspired many of us to think of new ways of experiencing our desire now.

- One client dreamed of having a spa in her house so she purchased some items from her favorite spa and created a "steam room" in her bathroom. Then she asked her partner to be her personal massage therapist. Not only did they have a lot of fun together, but within twelve months they moved into a new home with the most luxurious bathrooms, found an infrared sauna at a garage sale, and even met a friend who was getting her massage license and needed practice hours, so she would come to their house to massage her every week!

Get creative in finding a way to bring elements of your dream life to you, and before you know it, you will be living it!

Go on *Oprah*

So many people I know have a goal of being on *Oprah*, *Ellen*, or some other TV show. They see that kind of an appearance as the pinnacle of success because they know they wouldn't be on those shows unless they've done something extraordinary.

So during my MasterMind events, my team and I create a set of television show: *The Lana Show*. We have an audience, cameras, lights, chairs, flowers, a producer, and more, so it feels very real. I take the participants through a preparation process so that when the time comes, they walk out on the set of *The Lana Show* to talk about how they achieved their WOW dreams. I'm great at improv, so this appearance always takes their future reality into new directions they didn't expect and adds so much color, texture, meaning, and power to the vision.

This simulated-reality experience is always the one that the participants tell me changed their lives forever. It makes their vision real. They feel like they've already lived it. They get a video recording of it as evidence. Plus, they get to celebrate with everyone at the event as if it's already done and now they are focusing on what's next. Can you imagine the power of this kind of experience?

Now, if you can't make it to the set of *The Lana Show* at my events, think about how you can simulate this kind of experience for yourself. Get your friends involved, record videos, or role-play in any way that takes you to the heart of that vision. You will be amazed by the immediate impact it will have on how you view yourself and how you think about actions you can take toward accomplishing this goal.

Marry Yourself

Years ago, I said this to my boyfriend in a fit of fury: "If you love me, then why don't your actions reflect it? You say that you want to be together and have a family, but you haven't proposed and don't seem interested in making joint decisions in life together. I don't think you really love me. Or maybe you'll never be ready for commitment."

I so badly wanted someone to show me that I was worthy of unconditional love. I wanted men to prove to me that I was not broken and unwanted. But the truth is, no matter how hard any of them tried, they couldn't give me what I was seeking. No amount of flowers, romantic getaways, proclamations of eternal love, and post-coital embraces could prove to me that I was lovable, worthy, and whole.

When I recognized this pattern of looking for love in all the wrong places, I was horrified at how deeply this wounded and dissatisfying self-view ran through generations of my family. I could not stand the thought of passing it down to my future children.

I read many books, attended various self-help seminars, and practiced yoga and meditation – they all helped bring new perspectives on how to love and nurture myself. However, there was one defining day when my self-love affair became a committed union. On a sunny day in 2007, I walked into a Sunday service at Agape International Center a single woman. And I walked out a married one.

That day, the brilliant Rev. Michael Bernard Beckwith took each participant through a ceremony of marrying our Highest Selves. He invited us to recognize the primary relationship that all other relationships are built upon. If we don't commit to walking hand-in-hand with ourselves, then how do we expect to have that with others? If we don't marry our Higher Self, then we will never find what we are looking for in any human union.

The wisdom and poignancy of his words pierced to the very core of me. I had one of those *a-ha* moments that shook me at all levels. It awakened me to a new paradigm. I no longer felt the desire to base my life on finding "the one" to settle and have a family with. Because I had already found "him" – and it was me.

Rev. Michael asked us to take our own hands and repeat: "I, Lana, take you, My Highest Self, to be my partner. I promise to be true to you in good times and in bad. I will love you and honor you all the days of my life. I will take care of you and cherish you." The day I married myself in that center transformed the rest of my life. While relationships with others wax and wane, my matrimony to my God-self is ever-present. This is the marriage I've always wanted.

After I walked out of that service, I marched straight to the store at the center and asked them to show me their jewelry case. I selected three rings that called to me, laid them out on the counter, closed my eyes and glided my right hand over them, feeling for heat and tingles. I didn't look at the cost. I didn't choose the prettiest one. I let my Inner Wisdom choose the perfect one for me.

When I opened my eyes to see which one I selected, chills washed over me. It was a simple solid silver band with the word "Gratitude" engraved on the outer rim. It was the perfect wedding band. I put it on my left-hand ring finger and didn't take it off until almost two years later, when my now-husband replaced it with an engagement ring.

That band served as a daily reminder of my unwavering commitment to following my truth. My promise to live in alignment with my soul. I knew that this was a union that would always be my primary marriage. The only thing that was left was to throw myself a lovely dinner party celebrating my wedding!

I invited a few close friends, including my now-husband, to dinner. They all knew the reason for gathering and got in the spirit of the celebration by bringing gifts and cards! We laughed and cried and spoke poetic words of eternal love. This time, I believed it. I felt like I had finally found what I had been looking for: a partner in life who I could always count on, who always had my best interest in mind, and who loved me unconditionally.

I had arrived! I married a keeper, and this partner had been under my nose all along!

So whether you are in a committed relationship with someone or not, I hope you will consider entering a union between you and You. Buy yourself flowers, take yourself out to dinner, write love notes to yourself, put on your best lingerie and please yourself – in other words, treat yourself the way you'd want your perfect mate to treat you. Get ready to experience the magical ways that your self-love celebration will reverberate through your world and up-level and enrich all of your relationships. I know it has for me.

I married the man of my dreams in a sacred ceremony in Sedona in 2011. During the ceremony, my promise to him was to share the love I harvest in my primary relationship with my Higher Self. He promised the same. And even though I now wear my gorgeous vintage engagement ring (we're not the wedding band type of people), the energy and essence of my gratitude ring is still embodied in my ring finger. It forever reminds me of *the* union that is at the foundation for all of my relationships.

I chose self-love and I've never looked back. Now if you ask my children, "Who loves you the most?" they will instantly reply, "Myself." That makes me so incredibly proud.

So if you want to change generational patterns of feeling unloved, unwanted, and not enough, I hope you'll consider doing a simple ceremony where you marry yourself. I love officiating the Marry Yourself Ceremony as part of my programs and the participants rave about it. Many of my previous program participants said that this one experience changed their lives forevermore and allowed them to manifest unconditional self-love that attracted epic romantic love into their lives!

Miracle Practice – Embody

I hope these Creative Expression visioning ideas will inspire you to try out ways of simulating and embodying your desires so that they feel possible and certain. I also hope that this chapter reminds you that there are infinite ways for you to experience your key intentions and core desired feelings. You don't have to wait to win a million dollars in a lottery to test drive a car and feel wealthy today! You can harvest what you most desire today by using the incredible power of your imagination.

I hope that these fun right brain ways to play make your life a little more sparkly, exciting, magical, and pleasurable. Don't underestimate how powerful it is to travel parallel realities and be who you dream of being.

"Strong emotions such as passion and bliss are indications that you're connected to Spirit, or 'inspired,' if you will. When you're inspired, you activate dormant forces, and the abundance you seek in any form comes streaming into your life." — Wayne Dyer

When you can believe that all of life is rigged in your favor, it will show you that it is. The endless human and divine support that will show up in the most unexpected ways will certainly make you believe that truly, miracles are possible for those who know how to receive them! If you can manifest an Audi, dream home, unexpected money, or unconditional self-love, imagine how you can use the power of your mind to create a better world!

10:

Experiment and Evaluate

"Celebrations multiply manifestations!"
—Lana Shlafer

So many people achieve their goals, successes, and intentions, but forget to evaluate and celebrate. That's a huge missed opportunity to add even more fuel to your manifesting rocket! Plus, a huge part of concluding a process is evaluating what worked and what didn't, determining what can be done better next time, and reflecting on the results. Without taking the time to reflect on the experience, we won't learn from it and get more masterful at it.

As we come to the end of the Miracle Mindset process, this last step of evaluating and celebrating is hugely important. Let's look back on the time you've been doing the exercises in this book and reflect on what you've learned, how you've changed, and what you've manifested.

Evaluation Process

1. First, think about the things you learned from this book and from experimenting with the practices outlined here.
   - Were there any a-has, lightbulb moments, or new ideas? How did they change your perspective or life?
   - What were some of you favorite exercises or practices? Why did you love them and what results did you notice?
   - What were some of your least favorite practices and why? Are there some exercises you want to get better at?

2. Now consider how your life has changed:
   - How do you now view yourself and what's possible for you differently?
   - What shifts, breakthroughs, miracles, or manifestations have you seen?
   - How are you now different in the way you approach the ups, downs, and sideways of life?
   - Look back on your core intentions – how have they manifested in various areas of your life?
   - Look back on your WOW dreams – do you now feel closer to achieving them?
   - How have other people reflected to you that you've changed?

- Have your intentions, dreams, and visions evolved? If yes, how?

3. Let's consider what's next:
   - How can you continue to practice and apply what you learned in this book to get to the next level?
   - What opportunities to upgrade your mindset and up-level your life would you like to focus on next?
   - What kind of support do you need to make the shifts you've seen continue to stick and evolve?

The Wheel of Life Exercise – Revisited!

You completed the Wheel of Life exercise in Chapter 4. Now let's evaluate where you stand. Without looking at your previous answers, fill out the Wheel of Life about how you feel now about each area of life, then reflect on the questions below.

Reflection

1. How did it feel to do this exercise now versus when you did it before?

2. Take out the previous Wheel of Life assessment and compare the two versions. What differences do you notice with the Wheel overall?

3. In the areas where you noticed a difference, what do you attribute this change to? What practices, actions, or experiences created the change?

4. What improvement would you like to see in the Wheel of Life next? What tools and techniques from this book can you use to create these changes?

As you evaluate the practices you learned in this book, look for both inner results (improvement in how you feel) and outer results (changes in your life). There are no coincidences! So if you somehow "miraculously" got a new client or had a huge breakthrough with a family member, it's absolutely related to reading this book and trying out the practices. Even if you didn't directly focus on that specific situation or area, you can attribute it to the shift in your mindset, behavior, and attitude.

I hope you will take the time to sift through the qualitative and quantitative data and assess the evidence. It will not only prove to you that this stuff works, but it will greatly help you improve the effectiveness of these tools and make the Miracle Mindset your new normal! There have been so many clients who I've worked with who didn't really see the huge improvements and miracles in their lives until they did the Wheel of Life – Revisited exercise. Frequently, they were so focused on the one area of life they wanted to up-level that they didn't see how so many other areas had increased in satisfaction and fulfillment.

One of my clients really struggled through the Miracle Mindset processes and exercises and harshly compared herself with other participants who were seeing unbelievable results. It was disappointing for her to see others manifest amazing new jobs, incredible personal healings, and large sums of money while she was only seeing "incremental" improvements.

But after she did the Wheel of Life – Revisited exercise, she wrote to me in shock with grateful tears! She couldn't believe how much *everything* in her life up-leveled! She went from having no area of her Wheel being above level five and most areas being between two or three, to *all* areas of her life being above five, with most of them at seven or eight.

She is a classic example of someone not seeing the forest for the trees! Here she was thinking *the* miracle was going to be some huge manifestation like winning the lottery, but what she actually got was the biggest miracle of all. After forty years on this planet, for the first time she truly liked her life and felt safe, empowered, at peace, and in joy for a lot of her days. This seemed completely impossible to her before she began developing the Miracle Mindset!

After the Wheel of Life – Revisited exercise, she realized just how much inner healing she'd had and how much she'd given up generational patterns of being the martyr. The feeling of living in constant chaos – feeling that her kids were just unmanageable and difficult, that her husband was just unsupportive, that her job was just underpaid, and that her health was just always going to be awful – was now replaced with knowing that she created her own reality and was in charge of her life.

The fact that in mere months she was able to improve her health, feel more rested and vibrant, regain the passion and connection she had been craving in her marriage, feel as if her job got easier, and feel as though her kids were now a source of joy was a *miracle* that seemed more impossible than winning the lottery!

So I hope this reflection exercise gives you perspective on what has shifted, improved, and manifested in your life as a result of the mindset work you've done. Then you'll be ready for the next step of celebrating these breakthroughs and miracles!

Celebrate

Celebration is appreciation in action. It is one of the most under-rated manifesting techniques. Because whatever we praise, we raise!

You've just reflected on the shifts, breakthroughs, transformations, and manifestations you've seen through applying the principles and practices in this book. Now what are you going to do about it?! Time to jump with joy, have a party, and whoop it up! The act of acknowledging and appreciating how far you've come and what you've accomplished is the fastest way to attract more amazing manifestations.

If you don't acknowledge, feel grateful for, and celebrate the results that you have already seen, why would you want to receive more of them? So whether you've seen massive manifestations, powerful inner transformations, or even a small uptick in your well-being, let's praise the Lord – and yourself – for it! You don't have to have a once-in-a-lifetime success to pop open some champagne and do a happy dance!

Celebrating gets easier with practice, just like anything else. Here are some ideas for how to celebrate the Miracle Mindset process you've started to learn and acknowledge the results that you've seen.

Ways to Celebrate

- Get yourself dressed to the nines with your favorite clothes and accessories. Why delay feeling amazing and enjoying your favorite things when you can make today special? Take a hot selfie and enjoy being fabulous at home or out!

- Get a delicious mouth-watering dessert and savor every morsel! Or get your favorite drink, make sure it's in the fanciest glass or cup, and toast to yourself!

- Write a short love note to yourself about why you are awesome and proud of yourself! Why wait for someone else to praise you when you can celebrate yourself?

- Put on your favorite celebration song and either sing along as loud as you can or have a dance party... or both!

- Have a self-date! Schedule a date with yourself to do something that nourishes you! You could visit a spa, read an inspiring book, go to a fancy coffee shop, or make time for anything else that whisks you away into a feeling of celebration!

- Buy fresh plants or a beautiful decoration to brighten up your home! Or if you're feeling really frisky, order some flowers or chocolates to be delivered to you!

- Go for a walk or drive in a beautiful place, breathe in the fresh air, listen to the wind and the birds, or find some other way to add an element of extra magic to today!

- Do something that you used to love as a child. Hula hoop, jump rope, lie on the floor looking up at the ceiling, talk to your imaginary friend... anything that takes you back to the feeling of being young, free, and happy!

- Veg out! Sometimes the greatest gift we can give ourselves is the gift of free time to do a whole bunch of nothing! Let yourself lounge around, watch a rom com, or do whatever "guilty" pleasure you have without any guilt at all. A little bit of rest and play can go a long way!

- Buy that beautiful thing you've been eyeing that makes you feel abundant, special, and happy! It can be a bright lipstick, a fancy wallet, new soft bed sheets, colorful towels, or a ticket to a concert! Watch how you feeling good and spending on yourself attracts more celebrations in your life!

- Write a letter or note of thanks to someone who has supported you. Let them know how their support and wisdom has impacted you and how you are celebrating their presence in your life. Now you've got them on your celebration train too!

- Make love to a lover or yourself! Get those endorphins flowing! Nothing better than celebration orgasms!

- Write down the biggest success you've experienced so far and put it somewhere you can see every day. Doesn't matter if it's big or small. Why only celebrate it once when you can milk the high vibration over and over again to manifest more successes?

This list is just to give you ideas of how you can continue to add more celebration into your everyday life. My personal favorites are popping a bottle of bubbly, going out to a special meal, writing notes of appreciation for everyone who helped me on my way to the manifestation, and thinking of something spontaneous and fun to do that I haven't tried before!

I know that by celebrating what you have created, you'll feel more appreciation and attract *a lot* more of this goodness!

Are You Worthy?

The challenge for most people is to feel worthy of praise and celebration. Maybe you were taught it's inappropriate, boastful, or in bad taste. To that I say – are you crazy? If you are here feeling proud of yourself, appreciating what's going well, and uplifting everyone around you, how is that not public service 101?

Only those who are insecure, jealous, and overly concerned about what others think of them would consider joyous celebration unsavory. Those aren't friends you want to pay attention to! Instead, look for those who will encourage you to transcend the glass ceilings you may have unconsciously put in place for yourself. If you start to feel like you've reached a limit on how much goodness you can handle in your life, they'll be there to support you in surpassing these self-imposed limits to a more proud and bold you!

One of the best parts of my programs is the community we create of everyone lifting each other up and encouraging you to be full of yourself! After all, who else should you be full of? And when you can learn to celebrate the small daily things, you will build the muscle to welcome, receive, and enjoy the desires you've been longing for for a long time.

That's when you will no longer see any manifestation as big or small, because everything will feel possible and yet not needed. You won't need some big successes to feel worthy because you'll already feel great every day in your normal life. And that's the biggest success ever!

11:

Learn and Repeat

"Everything is hard before it is easy."
—Goethe J.W.

Maybe you've seen amazing results from trying out the processes in this book, or maybe you've found yourself not really making time for the practices, or feeling like the manifestations aren't coming as fast as you'd like. Either way, here is the truth: to see progress, you will need to keep practicing.

Any pro-athlete, acclaimed artist, innovative visionary, or CEO will tell you that consistency is what creates massive results. But it's really difficult to have consistency without support. Encouragement, guidance, mentorship, and inspiration are necessary in order to see upward momentum and reach big goals. Now that you have learned the ABCs of manifesting miracles, it's time to address what it will take to actually create masterpieces.

Practice, Practice, Practice

It's not enough to read this book and do the exercises once. If you can find the practices you enjoy and make them a part of your daily routine, you will start to see exponential improvement in your inner world and outer reality. It is through practicing that you will learn what works best for you and when. That's why, in my courses, we value getting it done versus getting it perfect. It's in tenacious exploration and persistent discovery that we find mastery.

In any great program, there is a huge emphasis on putting systems in place that create the consistent ability to show up and take the next step. This is why I have such a high completion rate in my programs, and why the participants see extraordinary results – no matter what is happening in their life, they have a safe and supportive place to show up as they are and be held accountable to keep doing the work.

Plus, when you feel guided, held, and encouraged in this mindset training, you will enjoy it so much more and want to practice daily. You'll be celebrating every step of the way and see so many others who are experiencing inspiring breakthroughs, massive shifts, and unbelievable manifestations!

The next level of manifesting mastery is to make these practices as normal as brushing your teeth every day. Feeding your visions and strengthening your realignment muscles will pay off in the kind of optimal vibrational health that will lead to miracle after miracle in your life!

Support, Support, Support

Even though you don't need anything but alignment with Source to manifest miracles, let's be real. It's a heck of a lot easier and faster to do it with others! The truth is most people will not get where they want to go by operating solo. You really do need a village – on the earth-plane as much as in the divine-realm. The good news is that there is *so* much assistance available to you in so many ways!

The majority of my clients didn't have family members or friends who were on the same wavelength, so they joined my programs, came to my events, or hired me as a coach. They knew the value of having someone who could hold them up when they were feeling down and encourage them to reach even further when they were soaring high.

When I first got into yoga, I went to teacher trainings and workshops, and developed a community of yoga teachers that supported me as I grew my yoga-teaching practice. It's the same with law of attraction – I've been to dozens of trainings, events, and Abraham-Hicks cruises. I have invested *a lot* of time, money, resources, and energy to create support for this new way of living. And boy have all of those investments come back to me tenfold! Frequently, I'd even manifest back the money I spent on a training in unexpected ways and within weeks.

That's what many of my program participants report, too – when they go to another vibrational level, their financial level raises without any real effort on their part. It's just what happens because an elevated mindset creates shifts that are the rising tide that lifts all boats! The value of learning from others who are on the same path is immeasurable. It's like multiplying the lessons and growth you'd have on your own by a thousand-fold.

Teamwork is what makes the dream work. As I look back on my life, I can see a clear correlation between how much mentorship, guidance, assistance, and support I invited in and the results that I saw. It took me a lifetime, but now I'm grateful to have the best village in the world, including:

- An incredible team to uphold and expand the programs I offer
- A publishing team to help me increase my impact
- A paid mentorship program where I get to learn from the best and brightest coaches, entrepreneurs, and visionaries
- A peer mastermind group where I am held accountable and receive clarity and inspiration weekly
- Friends, family, and community – all of whom are enrolled in my vision and mission and offer massive reinforcement and assistance!

Who is part of your village? If you don't have the right support, then create, invite, and invest in it!

Resistance, Resistance, Resistance

The brighter you turn up your light, the more shadows you will see. The more you venture outside of your comfort zone, the more discomfort you will face. The more alignment you create in your life, the more unbearable it will feel to be out of alignment and carry resistance.

Frankly, I could write a whole book about resistance and how to learn to befriend it and turn it into your ally. It's a paradigm shift out of the old-school "no pain, no gain" mentality and the hustle culture that's been all the rage the last few decades. How it became cool to work 100 hours a week and have an ulcer or a mental breakdown in your twenties, I'll never fully understand, especially because any successes you create by sacrificing your health, your family, or your soul are *never* worth it.

There is a huge difference between finding something that inspires you and putting the time, energy, focus, and labor into it. That's not hustle – that's devotion, and devotion requires tough choices. But, devotion isn't about sacrifice. It's about reverence, consistency, and passion.

So even though I spent the last few months fervently writing this book and spending less time with my kids and husband than usual, I don't see it as a sacrifice. I see it as a choice. I made that choice deliberately because writing this book and sharing this message with the world was starting to feel less like a want and more like a need. I couldn't hold it in anymore. It's like being forty weeks pregnant and knowing the baby needs to come *now*. That means your other priorities take a temporary back seat.

Mastering resistance is ultimately about stepping out of duality – right or wrong, easy or hard, me or you – and finding oneness.

When you resist resistance – when you fight your fears, doubts, and pain – you only increase the resistance. But when you love resistance – when you welcome challenges, contrast, and discomfort and get curious about them – you increase love. So when you align with what is and don't resist it, you find oneness. Then you see how every ounce of that resistance can serve you.

Then you feel peace because you know that nothing's gone wrong, and everything has gone right. You are able to receive the gifts in the challenges, pain, and contrast and see them as meaningful parts of your journey. There comes a deep recognition that the obstacles came to be the fuel you need to get you to your desired destination faster. That's when you are fully human and fully divine at the same time: sensitive, aware, emotional, and yet invincible, powerful, and free.

How you face resistance is the biggest determining factor of what you will achieve in your life. With every client I've ever worked with and every successful person I've interacted with, one thing is clear. How someone faces challenges is what determines how far they go and what they manifest. I've seen people face terminal illness, loss of a loved one, natural disasters, freak accidents, bankruptcy, divorce, miscarriages, stillbirth, you name it. What they went through may be horrible, painful, traumatic, and unthinkable, but that is not the end of their story.

If you *decide* to face everything in life with the attitude of, "This too shall pass and I will learn and grow from it," then you will become unstoppable.

If my client Amber could have two miscarriages and a stillborn at eight months and then use these processes to grieve, heal, and connect with her true intentions and desires, then so can you. One of the happiest moments of my life was seeing her miracle baby born healthy and well after she "miraculously" got pregnant during my program! She couldn't believe after all the years of infertility treatments and unthinkable losses she and her husband faced that this was something she could even dream about.

All things are possible, just often not in the way we expected or in the timing we wanted. There is nothing more that I love than helping my clients and course participants learn to embrace sacred resistance and use it to manifest their biggest desires! As you continue the journey of transformation, evolution, and advancement in your life, you may face some of these common types of resistance. These are the mental blocks and mindset limits that stand between wishing versus achieving any dream:

1. **Upper limits** – fear of success, an inner limit of how good things could get, self-sabotage, and regression.

2. **Lower limits** – fear of failure, stagnation, depression, denial, suppression, and powerlessness.

3. **Friendship limits** – fear of leaving others behind, savior complex, feeling alone, desperation, and regret.

4. **Partnership limits** – not knowing how to handle triggers, shame, blame, heartache, feeling broken, and unwanted.

5. **Money limits** – fear of lack, obsessive worry about spending, guilt, judgement, remorse, and feeling imprisoned.

6. **Time limits** – scarcity mentality, chronic insufficiency, feeling suffocated and depleted.

7. **Trust limits** – existential crisis, loss of meaning or purpose, skepticism, disbelief, depletion, and emptiness.

Just to be clear, some or all of these limits will come up at one point or another in everyone's life. But they will definitely take center stage as you go to the leading-edge. What determines success, and most importantly, fulfillment and happiness, isn't whether you manage to avoid these limits. It's actually about how well you can navigate these fears, inner challenges, and outer setbacks. Circumstances cannot keep the manifestation from coming, only your response to the circumstances can block it. When you learn that every note on the emotional keyboard is useful in composing a masterpiece, you become a skillful composer who can create hit after hit and miracle after miracle in your life.

A masterful race car driver isn't afraid of speed or the friction it causes. A pro knows how to use the brakes, gas, and gears to curve the road, hug the turns, and drive without spinning out. I've spent most of my entire personal and professional life learning how to navigate human experiences and emotions. I can promise you that it's not *what* is happening, but *how* you handle what is happening that will determine the outcome for that situation.

Honestly, when these blocks come up, I recommend doubling up on professional support around you – hire a coach or therapist, join a course, go to a workshop or a retreat. Invest time, energy, money, and focus on learning how to transcend limits as they arise. Because what's at stake isn't just a smaller house or feeling stuck in your job – it's dying with your dream in you. The real cost is getting to the end of your life and wishing you dared to do more.

Your desires, your goals, and your self-fulfillment aren't just some frivolous, nice-to-have destinations. *They are your destiny.* And you can't deny your destiny! But you can spend a lifetime suppressing it and feeling miserable. I hope this book is showing you that your visions and dreams are your divine mandate for this life, and that they are absolutely 100 percent possible and doable.

Remember: *Inspired Intention + Inspired Action = Miracles.* So keep visioning and following your inspiration step by step. You will be amazed at how far you can go in life! That's when you start to feel like you are truly a magician and anything that you hold in your mind, you will hold in your hand!

12:

Don't Forget to Celebrate

"There are two ways to live: you can live as if nothing is a miracle; you can live as if everything is a miracle."

—Albert Einstein

You've made it to the last chapter!

I'm guessing you've figured out by now that the real goal isn't to accomplish a bunch of goals or get a bunch of stuff. Maybe that's why you picked up this book. Maybe you wanted to figure out that missing piece of why you couldn't get what you wanted... and why you were never able to feel satisfied and truly fulfilled no matter the circumstances.

But I've done a little bit of a bait and switch on you! It's because I want to see you not just happy once, but truly fulfilled for a lifetime. We have covered so much ground in this book:

- We discussed what it takes to manifest beyond what you believe is possible – *Inspired Intention + Inspired Action = Miracles.*

- You committed to suspend your skepticism, try the Miracle Mindset tools, and assess for yourself whether they are effective or not in helping you identify and reach your true goals.

- You learned about me and why I'm so passionate about teaching these principles – I wasn't born with this knowledge and if I can create miraculous manifestations and a fulfilling life, so can anyone.

- We started with Step 1, to assess where you were in life and why you were there. I hope here you recognized what you truly want is to receive what you didn't get in childhood and courageously go after the key intentions and visions that are your destiny to fulfill in this lifetime.

- Step 2, Allow, was about recognizing that to go from problem to solution, and from vision to manifestation, you will need to expand your mindset and learn to turn your receptive mode *on*.

- In Step 3a, Imagine, you discovered the immense power of your imagination to create your reality and explored various ways of Creative Visioning to bring intentions to life.

- In Step 3b, Write, you explored how to use writing as a way to script your future and create a new version of yourself.

- In Step 3c, Speak, you learned the incredible power of your voice and using words to speak your visions into existence.

- In Step 3d, Create, you discovered ways to "act as in" your preferred reality and instantly embody what you desire.

- In Step 4, Evaluate, you reflected on what you've learned and what results you experienced by applying the techniques in this book. Plus, you understood the value of celebrating every shift and manifestation!

- Finally, you learned about the common blocks to making the Miracle Mindset work for you and what it takes to transcend them in order to consistently manifest miracles and feel better in your life.

I've shared with you as many exercises, practices, approaches, and tools as I could reasonably fit in a book (without making it 500 pages). I hope the personal experiences and client stories I included gave you a deeper understanding of the concepts and made you excited to know what's possible with consistent practice. I hope this book also showed you what's achievable for you and how to break through your inner limits to create true freedom, abundance, joy, love, and satisfaction in your life!

Now I want to leave you with a few final thoughts.

I wrote this book not for fame or money (though I am totally open to it!), I wrote it because the things I shared with you were so revolutionary in my life that I can't help but shout about them for everyone to hear. I've been "shouting" on my blog, through videos, podcasts, programs, and events for years. I saw thousands of lives change. So, I knew it was time to share what I have lived, learned, and taught with even more people in the world.

During the process of writing this book, all kinds of limits came up:

- Who am I and why would anyone want to read this book? What if what I write is misinterpreted and ridiculed? What if this book flops and I feel like a failure?
- When will I find time to dedicate to completing it? Who'll take care of the kids and run my programs?
- What if I just can't do it?

And so much more! When all of this resistance came up, I did exactly what I encourage you to do. I faced it and embraced it:

- So what if I fail? I just want to write and publish something I'm proud of and no one can take that away.
- So what if it takes me a long time to finish? I will keep showing up every step of the way until it's done. I will hire support to light a fire under my bum to get it done.
- So what if my kids and hubby get to go spend time with grandparents in California while I have a few weeks to write? I am not the Source of all love for them and they will benefit from spending time with others who love them!

I imagined a million times what it would be like to hold the book in my hands. I have probably spent close to a thousand hours over the years envisioning this book. I've written hundreds of visions detailing the impact it would make and how it felt. I've spoken to myself and others a gazillion times about what it would be like to be an author. I've created mock book release parties and even wrote the acknowledgements section of the book years ago to fully step into the feeling of it. I have used *every* tool in this book to turn receptive-mode on and create something that feels like a masterpiece.

Now it's here! You are holding it!

They say that one in three people dream of writing a book. Millions attempt and don't finish. Hundreds of thousands finish, but never publish or have their books reach more than a handful of people. The fact that you are holding this book is a miracle, and I can promise you it wasn't accidental. I've manifested this miracle consciously, systematically, and deliberately.

The non-physical support and the earth angels who've helped me – it was all on divine timing and truly beyond my imagination. But I was the one that called it forth. I followed Inspired Intention, put in a heck of a lot of Inspired Action, and created this miracle.

And so can you. Whether it sounds trite or not, it's the truth: you can create whatever you want. You hold the key to creating those realities. You hold the power to manifest miracles. Whether it's a book, a baby, a job, a physical healing, or finally feeling whole, lovable, and successful – it's yours for the taking!

I wish I could sit down with you over a cup of coffee and hear what you thought of this book. I wish I could personally hear your breakthroughs and manifestations through doing this work and also hear your frustrations and questions (if any). I've waited years to write this book because I didn't want it to be just another "manifestation lite," New Age, cliché, formulaic marketing ploy.

Of course, I can't control who loves or hates this book, or who gets results and who doesn't even try. That doesn't really matter anyway. I wrote this book for me and for those ready to deliberately mold their minds, create a new reality, and make miracles happen. I wrote it in devotion to everything I've learned, everything I've manifested, and everyone whose lives have transformed through working with me.

This book is proof that real miracles and extraordinary accomplishments are possible. I wanted to amplify this in the collective consciousness so that in my children's futures, there are more and more people who dream big and create the impossible.

As much as I tried to organize the Miracle Mindset into steps, real life is anything but linear. It is unexpected, uncontrollable, unpredictable, and no formula or system can work perfectly in it. What I've attempted to create with my body of work is a focus on building the kind of *you* who withstands the twists and turns of life and can rise up under any circumstances.

I wanted to write a book that honors, and even celebrates, the complexity, diversity, and chaos of life, and helps you navigate through uncharted territories with a clear destination and a map. I hope the words in these chapters radically improve your life. But most importantly, my wish for you is that you never again feel broken or beyond hope.

I wish for you to be able to make lemonade out of lemons. I wish for you to feel bigger than any problem. I wish for you to remember that you are a miracle simply by your existence.

Just think...

There are over seven billion people on the planet. There are around 250 million sperm cells in a male ejaculation and a woman carries one to two million eggs in her lifetime. What are the chances that a particular sperm fertilized a particular egg at just the right time to create you? Think of all the other ancestors, decisions, locations, and other infinite factors that played a role for you to be born to these parents, at this time.

It's as if all of earth's five billion year history led up to the moment you were born. Every natural phenomenon, every action, decision, occurrence, and experience was divinely orchestrated for you to come forth as *you*.

You, in all of your imperfection and uniqueness. There is no one in all of existence like you and never will be. It's easy to lose perspective and feel small, insignificant, and lost in such a big world. It's easy to lose sight of what you truly are. But here is the truth: you are a miracle – a supernatural occurrence that cannot be replicated or explained solely by science or logic. So as you think about manifesting miracles in your life, remember that the biggest miracle that you could ever create is already here. It's you.

I hope you spend the rest of your life discovering why in an act of divine grace you came forth on this plane of existence at this time. It's time for you to discover your purpose, live your big visions, and fulfill your destiny. All of creation is gleefully supporting you in manifesting miracles in your life – and there is a daring, fire-eyed, big-hearted Russian girl who is holding you in her heart and cheering you on from afar.

You've got this.

Life's got you.

Now go forth and manifest some epic miracles in this world!

Acknowledgments

I've spent a long time thinking about this section acknowledging the love, support, inspiration, encouragement, and assistance that I've graciously received. There has been so much!

I'd like to begin by thanking my ancestors who came before me. I stand on your shoulders and I hear your voices offering support at times when I need it most. You may not be visible, but you are real to me. Thank you for reminding me that I'm the answer to your prayers. Thank you for being the wind beneath my wings as I dare soar higher than ever before.

I am forever indebted to my mom, Irene Shlafer, and my dad, Alexander Shlafer, for always supporting me. I know you don't always understand me, but I know you always love me. I hope to make you proud not just by what I accomplish, but by who I become. I know I won the divine lottery by being your daughter. Thank you for coming to Puerto Rico to watch the kids so I could bring this book to life. Without your support, I wouldn't be here and I'm eternally grateful. You are my greatest inspiration!

To my husband, Francis – honey, where do I begin? I love you infinitely and there is no one I'd rather take insane risks with or manifest miracles with. I have always been grateful for your rock-steady support and the way we are a true team in our family, but during the writing of this book you really showed up in unprecedented ways. Thank you for always believing in me and encouraging me to dream big and leap far. You are my greatest manifestation!

To my kiddos, Mimi, Zaanti, and Haelan – you are my why. Before you were even born you inspired me to grow, learn, and create a new paradigm. Since becoming your mama, I've learned more from you than anyone else. You are master manifestors! Thank you for bringing me snacks and being so understanding during the times I was cooped up in my office writing this book instead of out with you and daddy. You are my greatest miracles!

To my extended family and friends, thank you for all the encouragement over the years to write this book. Thank you for holding the vision with me and being an amazing part of bringing it to life. Doyle Smiens, Siva Mohan, Tobi Mueller, Lily, Nichols, Sarah Grear, Tina Devine, Amanda Rodd, Palmas Wolfpack (Heidi, Selena, Krista, Kate, Cora, Arleen), and so many more – thank you! It takes a village and you are the best village!

To all of the people that have been part of Team Lana in my company – thank you for believing in this mission and dedicating your time, energy and talent to making miracles the new normal. Thank you for believing in me and serving our community in such a powerful way. Teamwork makes the dream work. You are the greatest dream team I can imagine!

To my publishing team at Difference Press headed by Angela Lauria, thank you for making this book possible. Without your constant support, brilliant guidance, expert advice, and creative direction, this manuscript would not see the light of day. You are my book angels!

To my teachers, mentors, and coaches, thank you for shining your light so bright that it helped me turn mine up. Thank you for paving the way so those like me can have a platform and a voice. You are the giants whose shoulders I stand on!

To my clients, program participants, and students – you are the reason this book exists. It was working with you and seeing your epic results and miracles that made me want to shout from the rooftops just how powerful and limitless we all are. I am a teacher among teachers and a master among masters. You are my greatest gifts!

And last but not least I want to thank myself. For all the times I showed up rain or shine to work on this book. For the way I held space and supported myself through the process of birthing this manuscript. For all the ballsy moves I made in my life that seemed crazy... Turns out I am crazy – I'm crazy enough to dream the impossible and make miracles happen!

In closing, I'd like to thank you, dear reader, for reading this book. I hope it reminds you that you can be crazy enough to believe that you are magic and that you can Manifest that Miracle!

Thank You

Thank you for reading this book. I would love to offer you a free, sixty-minute class so you can begin manifesting miracles daily. To get your access, go to www.lanashlafer.com/book-class

About the Author

Lana Shlafer is a mindset coach, law of attraction expert, and best-selling author. She studied at UC Berkeley and the Institute of Transpersonal Psychology. She is also a trained success coach and yoga teacher (RYT 500).

After the home birth of her twins (born thirty-three hours apart) and other extraordinary manifestations, Lana realized her passion didn't lie in being a therapist. Instead, she wanted to share how to use the law of attraction and mindset techniques to deliberately create unimaginable experiences and personal mastery.

Lana started her online coaching business in 2012 and built a thriving company that offers both online programs and live events. She has been featured on television and by popular publications such as *Forbes*, TVOne, and NPR.

Lana has empowered thousands of clients and students to experience what seems out of reach, including buying their dream home, healing from a chronic illness, and meeting their ideal partner. Over 20,000 people have joined her Manifesting Challenges and have experienced extraordinary breakthroughs and manifestations.

She resides in Puerto Rico with her three kids and husband, and is working on her second book.

Website: www.lanashlafer.com

CPSIA information can be obtained
at www.ICGtesting.com
Printed in the USA
JSHW041255060121
10708JS00004B/4